ALSO BY JOHN ARDOIN

The Stages of Menotti

The Callas Legacy

Callas
(with Gerald Fitzgerald)

CALLAS
AT JUILLIARD

CALLAS
AT JUILLIARD

The Master Classes

by JOHN ARDOIN

First published in Great Britain in 1988 by Robson Books Ltd,
Bolsover House, 5–6 Clipstone Street, London W1P 7EB.

Copyright © 1987 by John Ardoin

British Library Cataloguing in Publication Data

Callas, Maria
    Callas at Juilliard : the master classes.
    1. Opera. Arias. Performance.
    Interpretation
    I. Title   II. Ardoin, John
    782.1

ISBN 0–86051–504–4

Printed and bound by Adlard & Son Ltd.
The Garden City Press, Letchworth, Herts.

For two who went to Juilliard,

Shirley Verrett

and

John Woods

CONTENTS

Foreword by Nicola Rescigno   xi

Introduction   xv

PROLOGUE   3

THE CLASSES   13

MOZART   *Don Giovanni:* "Non mi dir"   15
Così fan tutte: "Come scoglio"   18
Die Zauberflöte: "O zitt're nicht"   21
"Der Hölle Rache"   24
"Ach, ich fühl's"   27

BEETHOVEN   "Ah! perfido"   28
Fidelio: "Abscheulicher!"   34

CHERUBINI   *Medea:* "Dei tuoi figli"   39

SPONTINI   *La vestale:* "Tu che invoco"   44

ROSSINI   *Il barbiere di Siviglia:* "Una voce poco fa"   50
La cenerentola: "Nacqui all'affanno"   57
Guglielmo Tell: "Selva opaca"   63

BELLINI   *Il pirata:* "Col sorriso d'innocenza"   67
La sonnambula: "Tutto è gioia"   76
"Come per me sereno"   77
Norma: "Casta diva"   81
"Sgombra è la sacra selva"   85
"Va, crudele"   86

I puritani: "Ah! per sempre" 89
"A te, o cara" 91
"Qui la voce" 92

DONIZETTI   *Lucia di Lammermoor:* "Regnava nel silenzio" 99
"Il pallor funesto" 106

Anna Bolena: "Al dolce guidami" 115

Don Pasquale: "Quel guardo il cavaliere" 121

VERDI   *Nabucco:* "Tu sul labbro" 127

Ernani: "Ernani, involami" 129

La battaglia di Legnano: "Quante volte" 132

Rigoletto: "È il sol dell'anima" 134
"Caro nome" 142
"Cortigiani, vil razza dannata" 147
"Tutte le feste . . . Piangi, fanciulla . . .
Sì, vendetta" 151

Il trovatore: "Stride la vampa" and "Condotta ell'era
in ceppi" 157
"Il balen del suo sorriso" 160

La traviata: "Ah! fors'è lui . . . Sempre libera" 162
"Addio del passato" 167

I vespri siciliani: "O tu, Palermo" 169

Simon Boccanegra: "Il lacerato spirito" 173

Un ballo in maschera: "Eri tu" 175

La forza del destino: "Me pellegrina ed orfana" 178
"Madre, pietosa Vergine" 182
"O tu che in seno agli angeli" 187

Don Carlo: "Nei giardin del bello" 191
"Ella giammai m'amò" 193
"Tu che le vanità" 197

Aida: "L'abborrita rivale" 203

Otello: "Credo" 208
Willow Song 212

BERLIOZ   *La damnation de Faust:*
"D'amour l'ardente flamme" 216

GOUNOD   *Faust:* Jewel Song 220

Roméo et Juliette: "Je veux vivre" 222

BIZET   *Carmen:* "Je dis que rien ne m'épouvante"   226

MASSENET   *Werther:* Air des lettres   229
            "Pourquoi me réveiller"   234

PONCHIELLI   *La gioconda:* "Stella del marinar!"   236

BOITO   *Mefistofele:* "L'altra notte"   239

LEONCAVALLO   *I pagliacci:* Prologo   242
               Ballatella   246
               "Vesti la giubba"   250

MASCAGNI   *Cavalleria rusticana:* "Tu qui, Santuzza?"   253

PUCCINI   *Manon Lescaut:* "Guardate, pazzo son"   264
           "Sola, perduta, abbandonata"   266

          La bohème: "Che gelida manina"   269
           "Sì, mi chiamano Mimì"   271
           "Quando me'n vo'"   275
           "Donde lieta uscì"   278
           "Vecchia zimarra"   280
           "Sono andati?"   281

          Tosca: "Recondita armonia"   284

          Madama Butterfly: "Che tua madre"   286

GIORDANO   *Andrea Chénier:* "Nemico della patria"   290

CILÈA   *Adriana Lecouvreur:* "Io son l'umile ancella"   292
         "Acerba voluttà"   294

EPILOGUE   297

Glossary   299

FOREWORD

This is a book about tradition—a way of performing opera that goes beyond the printed page. It has come down to us by word of mouth and practice, often from the composer himself. For the first time, apart from Luigi Ricci's important collection of cadenzas and embellishments, this oral heritage is documented in print as practiced by one of its major exponents, Maria Callas. This book is important not only because of what Callas stood for musically but because we are in danger of losing these traditions. They are still available to singers, but "tradition" has become almost a dirty word.

This has happened, I firmly believe, because of the many atrocities committed in recent years in the name of tradition: making an effect at the expense of a piece of music; over-ornamentation of an aria to a point where it is no longer recognizable; the insistence on setting aside traditional cuts which have been arrived at through performances over the years and which strengthen the drama and the musical structure of a work.

Because of abuses of tradition, some have jumped to the conclusion that all tradition is bad. This, of course, is not the case. What is bad is not studying or understanding the reasons for traditional practices. In many cases, cuts were either made by the composer or sanctioned by him as an opera was being rehearsed for its premiere. The same is true of changes in the vocal lines not found in the printed score. Composers such as Rossini, Bellini, and Donizetti tailored their music for specific singers, emphasizing their strengths and avoiding their weaknesses. When different singers took over the same music, alterations were made to accommodate their virtues and their limitations. This means that there was a great flexibility in the approach and performance of the bel canto operas in particular, for which Callas was so renowned.

Beyond this, there is the whole abstract way of feeling and responding to a piece of music which is beyond the power of musical notation. I remember reading of a famous instance when Verdi requested the broadening of a phrase during the rehearsal of one of his operas. Someone asked him, 'But, Maestro, why don't you write a ritard into the phrase?" "Because," Verdi responded,

"I only want a slight change in the tempo. I take it for granted a sensitive musician will understand this. If I write in 'ritard,' some imbecile will go from allegro to andante and ruin the phrase."

Much of the good in operatic tradition was created as well by great conductors, many of whom shaped Callas's thinking. They helped to make music live because they were willing to go beyond the printed page to reach the spirit of a piece. In law, every case is a little different from every other; yet all are tried under the same laws. Thus, a good law is one that has a broad application. So it is in music, where we have, as in the legal world, unwritten laws which have the power of law. Naturally, extremes must be avoided. They were not allowed by such conductors as Tullio Serafin, Victor de Sabata, and Arturo Toscanini. Yet each of these men had an individual approach to music: thus, we had equally historic but different performances of *Lucia di Lammermoor* by Toscanini and Toti dal Monte and by Serafin and Callas.

Throughout this book, you will find Callas speaking of good and bad tradition. You will also find that when she advocates a change in the music it is not for the sake of virtuosity but to bring out the intention of the composer. The constant quest of her studies was to realize fully the union of the word and the note. When I say "word," I also mean the dramatic development of a character from scene to scene through the use of the *sung* word. In this she was totally committed and uncompromising.

Callas was an extremely daring and courageous performer, who often courted disaster in order to achieve vocal and dramatic verity. I recall a series of *Traviata*s we did together at Covent Garden in 1958. Night after night she would sing an almost impossibly piano and disembodied A at the end of 'Addio del passato," not for the sake of a beautiful soft tone but because that was the only way to convey Violetta's *stato d'animo* at that moment. Occasionally the note was not perfectly secure, but she could not bring herself to compromise by singing it slightly more forte.

Callas has very often been accused of having three voices. Nonsense! She had three hundred. Every role she portrayed had a special voice, and within that particular timbre she would constantly change colors to convey the message of the composer. You will read in this book what pains she took to stress a word or even a syllable, and what miracles of technique she employed to achieve this end. She carefully built each of her personages on the one principal characteristic of the character's personality, not her own.

Medea was an extremely passionate woman, and to that passion she sacrificed all, even her children. Norma had the same passion, but she was capable of repentance. On these very simple facts Callas created two unforgettable, distinct portrayals of basically the same type of woman. Violetta was a courtesan, but within her soul were firmly embedded the seeds of greatness and nobility. Lucia, a sick girl, is doomed from the very start.

Once Maria had established in her mind the keynote to the character, she developed it with every possible means: the use of her voice, through which words took on myriad nuances (even her breathing was not a simple intake of air but could be a sigh, a laugh, a groan, or a snicker); the use of makeup, bodily attitudes, the superb handling of a costume or a cape to achieve certain effects, etc. On these bases she created her astounding gallery of portrayals: Lady Macbeth, Amina, Elvira, Leonora, Anna Bolena, Tosca, Iphigénie, Alceste, Elisabetta, Fiorilla, Lucia, and all the others.

I do not doubt that the natural talent of Callas was immense, but she perfected this gift with a great deal of study, discipline, and humility. I realize that humility is not a virtue one usually associates with the Callas personality. On the contrary, Maria, as an artist, was extremely humble. She was always the first to arrive at rehearsals and the last to leave, because of her eagerness to learn. She always sang full voice in order to arrive at the performance completely secure vocally. I recall a rehearsal of *Medea* in Dallas which lasted from seven p.m. to two a.m. After about four hours I suggested she "mark" rather than sing out. She politely told me to mind my own business, conducting, while she would mind hers. She completed the rehearsal in full voice.

Callas had completely freed herself of all the limitations singers usually impose on their acting: they can't kneel because it is difficult to get up gracefully; they can't bend because it decreases the capacity of the diaphragm; they won't take certain positions on stage because they have to watch the conductor or prompter constantly. During these *Medea* rehearsals, Maria asked her stage director, Alexis Minotis, to give her the same directions he had given his wife, Katina Paxinou, the great classical tragedienne. When he countered that the directions had to be different because of the singing involved, she told him, quite emphatically, to disregard that fact and direct her as freely as if it were a play. She felt it was her professional duty not to sacrifice acting to singing, or vice versa.

The greatest mark of Maria's humility was her subjection to the ultimate authority: the composer himself. She never sacrificed his intentions and indications to suit her gifts but rather put them at his complete service. This took a lifetime of hard work. One has to travel the road fully—there are no shortcuts in art. The old Latin adage "Festina lente" ("Be in a hurry slowly") should be the golden rule of every person who aspires to be an artist.

The musical examples in these pages are of great use to a singer, no doubt. But the important message of these lectures is the uncompromising artistic credo of Maria Callas; it shines through every word she spoke and every note she sang. She will be remembered not only as a great musician and artist but also as a great teacher.

Nicola Rescigno
New York City, 1987

INTRODUCTION

More than any other singer of this century, Maria Callas (1923–1977) exerted a dominant influence on the Italian operatic repertory and style of performance in our time. Even the most vehement detractors of her voice acknowledged this influence and the awesome range of her musicality. Indeed, Callas was not just a singer but a musician whose instrument was the voice.

After over fifteen years of appearances in the major opera houses of the world, Callas went into voluntary retirement in 1965 to work on her voice (beginning anew like a student) and reflect on questions of interpretation. A few years later, eager to share her feelings and findings, she accepted an invitation from Peter Mennin, then president of the Juilliard School of Music in New York City, to work with a select group of young professionals in a series of master classes in "The Lyric Tradition."

Out of three hundred applicants, twenty-five singers were chosen by audition to profit from Callas's instruction. For twelve weeks, two sessions a week, between October 1971 and March 1972, the singers took turns performing music from the standard repertory for Callas. Scenes and arias were heard ranging from Mozart's *Die Zauberflöte* to excerpts from all three periods of Verdi's writing, through romantic French composers into such twentieth-century operas as Puccini's *Turandot* and Cilèa's *L'Arlesiana*. Under her probing direction, scores were often dissected bar by bar in order to establish their dramatic premise and how best a sense of the music's drama could be achieved within a musical framework.

Callas labored not to produce a series of 'mini Callases" but to bring out the individual personalities and gifts of each singer. In doing so, she gave not only her views but possible alternatives as well. She adamantly insisted, however, that her students remain faithful to the style of a given piece, and she carefully explained of what this style consisted. She did this by delving into the text and its emotions, usually correlating the drama to an aria's musical substance. Callas rarely said "Do this" but rather said "Do this *because . . .* ," giving musical, theatrical, and historical reasons for her approach to the music.

In the extensive press coverage given the classes, one writer described the singer as "presiding like a Delphic oracle" before sold-out audiences of other students, fans, the musical press, and luminaries from the world of the performing arts who included Franco Zeffirelli, Lillian Gish, Ben Gazzara, Tito Gobbi, Elisabeth Schwarzkopf, and Bidù Sayão. Other artists, such as Patricia Brooks of the New York City Opera, were seen, scores in hand, paying rapt attention to the discussion.

Not only were Callas's comments extraordinary insights into her training and thinking, but they were a virtual summing up of a grand-line operatic tradition reaching back to Donizetti, Verdi, and beyond, which she had learned and practiced under such conducting giants as Tullio Serafin and Victor de Sabata. It is a tradition of which Callas was not only a principal exponent but one of the last of the breed.

This book, I hope, will act as a guide through major sections of the standard repertory for both professional singers and students as well as teachers. Here can be studied the means of creating drama through music, as well as the principles of bel canto and the stylistic nature of Mozart, Beethoven, Bellini, the French school, and the verismo epoch from an epic interpreter of this repertory. Several arias performed during the classes have been omitted here, because either Callas did not delve into the interpretative side of the music, the student was not well, or time ran out after a beginning was made and the particular aria was not brought to class again. However, the principles of a certain style can usually be applied to other works by the same composer.

It would not be stretching a point to say that the principles of performance Callas stressed have validity for instrumentalists as well. Any conscientious pianist or string player strives for a singing sound and for the naturalness of phrase that characterizes great singing. It was Chopin, after all, who urged his students to attend performances by Henrietta Sontag and Giuditta Pasta to understand better how his music should be performed, and instrumentalists down through the centuries to Vladimir Horowitz have conducted lifelong affairs with the art of singing.

Producing *Callas at Juilliard: The Master Classes* was far more than a matter of providing a literal transcription of what went on in the classes, for many of Callas's most penetrating "remarks" were sung rather than spoken. The points made through vocal examples had to be interpreted and translated into words. This meant listening "between the lines" to what was sung and supplying the reasons for many musical points when not given or fleshed out. Furthermore, as many of Callas's remarks were directed to the specific problems of a specific singer, they had to be adapted to fit the problems that singers in general would face when beginning work on the arias studied and discussed at Juilliard.

In presenting Callas's ideas, I have tried to keep her words when possible, but at times foreign-language expressions and musical terms had to be converted into English, thoughts had to be paraphrased, clarified, and above all organized into a concise flow. This was especially true where the same aria was performed by different students in different classes. Also, in order to point up the text and to avoid confusion as to specific phrases being discussed, a large number of musical examples have been included. These are usually presented *not* as they appear in a score but as they should be interpreted. Therefore, an example should be compared with the original to understand fully the performance practices involved. Here, too, will be found in print for the first time many of Callas's own cadenzas for bel canto operas. A keen reader will also find several instances where Callas changed her interpretative ideas between the time she recorded an aria and when she taught the same aria at Juilliard.

I have created a prologue for the book from general remarks made during the classes and from interviews given myself and others. In this prologue Callas deals with a wide range of subjects, from her early training with Elvira de Hidalgo to her own feelings concerning her voice and career. I felt the text here and throughout would be less cumbersome and more to the point if structured around Callas's words rather than set in mine.

Many helped and advised during the writing of this book, but I am particularly indebted to Nicola Rescigno. A longtime collaborator and friend of Callas's, he recorded extensively with her and conducted her American debut in 1954 as Norma in Chicago. He not only contributed a thoughtful foreword to this book but generously read the entire manuscript, checked the musical examples, and uncovered slips that might otherwise have gone uncorrected. This was of inestimable value, not only as Rescigno is a leading practitioner of the same tradition from which Callas sprang but because he is as highly regarded as a vocal authority as he is as a conductor. I am also exceedingly grateful to Callas's sister, Yacinthy Stathopoulou-Calogeropoulou, for her generosity in giving permission to use tape recordings of the classes as a basis for this book, and to Morgan Lowry, for his superb copying of the music examples.

Callas at Juilliard: The Master Classes is Callas on Callas, and Callas on music and on creating drama out of music. It complements rather than competes with my previous two books about this fascinating artist by unfolding in detail how she reacted to a score and her mental processes involved in bringing a piece of music to life. Once Callas said to me, "When it comes to music, we are all students, all our lives." Only the most serious and conscientious student can also be a teacher. Maria Callas was such a student.

John Ardoin
Dallas, 1987

CALLAS
AT JUILLIARD

PROLOGUE

"I started my vocal training early, as did my teacher Elvira de Hidalgo. In general, I think women tend to start early. Remember, too, I am Greek and de Hidalgo is Spanish. This means we are Mediterraneans; girls of this region grow up and mature earlier. A singer's career is essentially built on youth; wisdom comes later. Unfortunately, we cannot go on as long as conductors, for example. The earlier we receive our training, the better, so that we have the basis to acquire wisdom sooner.

"De Hidalgo had the real bel canto schooling; perhaps hers was the last of this great training. As a young girl, only thirteen, I was thrown into her arms to learn the secrets, the manner of bel canto. This training is not just 'beautiful singing'; that is a literal translation. Rather, bel canto is a method of singing, a sort of straitjacket you must put on. You learn how to approach a note, how to attack it, how to form a legato, how to create a mood, how to breathe so that there is a feeling of only a beginning and ending. In between, it must seem as if you have taken only one big breath, though in actuality there will be many phrases with many little breaths.

"Above all, bel canto is expression. A beautiful sound alone is not enough. For example, to make pasta you must have flour; that is the basic thing. Afterwards, you add other ingredients, plus knowhow, and shape the whole into something delicious. With a singer, we go to the conservatory for our basics. The training one receives there is crucial. If you start right, you are right for life. But if you start wrong, it is hard later to correct bad habits.

"After the conservatory, you make music with what you have learned. So, I repeat, it is not enough to have only a beautiful voice. You must take that voice and break it up into a thousand pieces so that it can be made to serve the needs of music, of expression. A composer has written the notes for you, but a singer must read music into them. Actually, we go by very little. Aren't there certain books that must be read between the lines in order to have their full meaning? Singers must do the same with their scores; we must add what the composer would have wanted, a thousand colors and expressions.

"Imagine how boring Jascha Heifetz would have been if he were only a wonderful technician. He is a great violinist because he goes beyond the notes. For a singer, this is even more important, because we have words as well as notes. We must do everything an instrumentalist does, plus more. It is very serious and difficult work, and it is not done out of our bravura or by willpower alone, but out of love, a devotion to what you adore. That is the strongest reason for anything.

"I must say that for me it was not really hard work. I suppose I was always a solitary girl; music was the main thing I loved. Whatever concerned music fascinated me. In Athens, I used to listen to all of de Hidalgo's pupils singing all sorts of repertory: light operas, heavy operas, arias for mezzo-sopranos, tenors. I was at the conservatory at ten in the morning and left with the last students. Even de Hidalgo was amazed at this. She frequently asked me, 'Why do you stay here?' My answer was that there was something to learn from even the least talented pupil, just as a great ballet dancer might learn from a cabaret artist.

"This way of thinking and behaving was set early in my life, not by me but by my family—my mother mainly, who was in command of the family. She had decided that I should become a singer, an artist. Parents say, 'I sacrificed myself for you; now you must do what I was supposed to do in life.' Anyway, this is the way it was with my mother. She also taught me as a child not to indulge in emotions unless it was absolutely necessary, though by nature I think I tended to be that way. I remember my father would take me walking, and if we passed an ice cream parlor, I would stop and pull his jacket, not saying a word. Then, I'd look at him, not at the ice cream parlor. He caught on after a while, but we continued to play our comedy. He would say, 'Just what is it you want, Maria?' I wouldn't answer; I just looked at him. That was my way then, as it was later in the theater.

"My mother and I went to Athens when I was thirteen. The plan at first was that I should only study and not sing professionally. This did not last long, for after six months with de Hidalgo, I was engaged by the National Theater. They needed a dramatic soprano and took me for one year on the proviso that I would not sing anywhere else. De Hidalgo saw to that in the contract. The money I earned at the opera enabled me to study full-time and not have to work.

"I had already sung *Cavalleria rusticana* and *Suor Angelica* at the conservatory; *Tosca* came about a year and a half after I joined the opera. These are heavy roles for a young girl, but de Hidalgo taught me that no matter how heavy the part, a voice must be kept light, never overweighted, and limber like an athlete's body. I also enjoyed working for this lightness, because it had always amused me to conquer a difficulty. I like challenge. How nice it is to master a problem and present it to the public with a maximum of ease.

"This lightness I sought was not only a part of the bel canto training de Hidalgo gave me: it was a part of her philosophy that a voice must be put into a zone where it will not be too large in sound, but nonetheless penetrating. This approach also made it easier to master all the bel canto embellishments —a vast language on its own. A singer conquers these difficulties just as an instrumentalist must, beginning first with slow scales and arpeggios, then gradually building up speed and flexibility. These are things which cannot be learned once you are on the stage; it is too late then. These so-called 'tricks' are not tricks at all but exercises like those an athlete does to build strength, endurance, and muscles. It is a lifetime's work. Not only does it never stop, but the more you learn, the more you realize how little you know. There are always new problems, new difficulties; more passion and love are needed for what you are doing.

"My performances in Greece were a sort of early, preparatory period, the completion, so to speak, of my school days. There I learned how far I could go and what my possibilities were. It is after your school days that you become a musician, that you put your instrument to the service of music. Remember, the voice is the first instrument of the orchestra. 'Prima donna' means just that —'first woman,' the main instrument of the performance. This I learned from Tullio Serafin. One of the luckiest things that ever happened to me, perhaps the luckiest, was to have him conduct my Italian debut—Verona, 1947, the beginning of my real career.

"What you got from that man! He taught me that there must be an expression to everything you do, a justification. I learned that every embellishment must be put to the service of music, and that if you really care for the composer and not just for your own personal success, you will always find the meaning of a trill or a scale that will justify a feeling of happiness, anxiety, sadness. Maestro Serafin taught me, in short, the depth of music. I drank all I could from him. He was the first of this kind of maestro I had, and I'm afraid the last. He showed me music is so enormous that unless you know what you are doing and why, it can envelop you in a state of perpetual anxiety and torture.

"He had a reason for everything. Serafin said, and this impressed me most, 'When one wants to find a gesture or how to move on stage, all you have to do is search for it in the score; the composer has already put it into his music.' How right he was, for if you take the trouble to listen with your whole soul and your ears—the mind must also work, but not too much—you will find everything you need. He also taught me that opera must be a single reflex of singing and acting, that a performance is simply many reflexes put together. But you only achieve this if you have done your homework well. When you reach the stage, there must be no surprises.

"Music was all the acting training I ever had. It is true I had coaching from de Hidalgo to achieve a continuously flowing line with my body; she gave me exercises for this and even taught me how to fall down without hurting myself, an important thing for the stage. However, much later I asked de Hidalgo if acting had been natural to me as a student. 'Yes,' she said, 'amazingly so. I always admired the way you moved your hands even then, and the ease of your body. Your way was new to me. I knew at once there was something different about it, something your own.'

"I remember, too, some good advice I had from a director at the National Theater: 'Never move your hand unless you follow it with your mind and soul.' That's a strange way of putting it, but it is so true. Movement must hang by the strings of your heart and mind. This director had probably said the same thing to others, but they had not made it their own. But I am a sponge. I love to grasp what others say and take from it what is good for me.

"Another thing this director told me was, 'When a colleague sings to you, try to forget the rehearsals; make your reactions seem as though you are hearing what he is saying for the first time.' I became able to do this to such an extent that if a colleague forgot his words, I couldn't give them to him. Theater has to be real; there must always be something new. It is like your signature; no two are the same, yet it is always yours. The same elasticity must be in art, in music, but only up to a certain point. There is always a limit. There must also be a rhythm to movement as well as to music. Everything must be measured. A high note cannot just be stupidly held. Everything is planned within a composer's style. And what is style? It is simply good taste.

"After my debut with Serafin in Italy, I had very few engagements. I was something new to listen to and my voice disturbed people, my interpretations made them work a little harder, feel a little more. They couldn't just hear me and say, 'Oh, what a lovely voice! . . . Oh, what a lovely note! . . . Oh, how nice, how pleasant—let's go home.' I even had colleagues who said, 'We were doing fine until she came along; now we have to work doubly hard.' I've caused, I must say, a bit of change in our art.

"Perhaps I should have gotten a press agent in those days when no one took notice of me. I have probably paid the consequences since for not hiring one. After all, art is not all beauty. But I'm a very independent creature and like to have what is due me—good or bad—the sincere way. The public must applaud me and love me as I am; otherwise, I don't think a career is worth it.

"I was disliked in the beginning because I took the public away from what was the tradition they knew, and not a very good one. But as I became better known, agents would come to me and say, 'Such-and-such a theater wants you.' I answered, 'Thank you very much, but they have already contacted me; I do not need to go through you.' That caused a lot of trouble, even to the booing of me in the theater. You see, agents like to have a big star because it allows them to pass off their lesser artists to theaters who want the star. But what has this to do with art?

"The way I got roles was to sing parts for which they couldn't find other singers. A young artist frequently has to do certain roles to get a contract, roles they might not be interested in or feel a sympathy for. Even so, I sang only every four or five months at first. When I did manage to get on the stage—whether it was as Turandot or as Aida—there were those who said, 'Well, her high notes are beautiful, but the low ones are no good.' Others said, 'Well, the middle notes are beautiful, but the top is bad.' No one agreed. What did impress me, however, was that they all said, 'She does know how to move on stage.'

"It was Serafin who got my career going. The fall after my debut in Verona, he needed an Isolde in Venice and asked for me. I didn't know the part, but I was so desperate to sing I said I did. An appointment was made, and I sight-read the second act for him. It went well. Afterwards, I confessed that I was only reading and didn't know the role. 'So what,' Serafin said. 'All you need is two months' work.' I remember, too, he insisted that I have special costumes made for Isolde, and this was when I really could not afford them. 'Why,' I asked him, 'is this so necessary?' 'The first act of *Tristan* is ninety minutes long, and no matter how much you fascinate the public with your voice, they still have all that time to look you over and cut your costume to pieces. So your appearance on stage must be harmonious with the music.'

"The next year Serafin asked me back to Venice to sing *La Walkiria;* at that time, we did the Wagner works in Italian, for the public would not accept them in German. Serafin was also conducting *Puritani* during the same weeks, and a great flu epidemic caused his soprano to become ill. Mrs. Serafin, hearing me singing 'Qui la voce,' which I used as a vocalise, begged me to sing it for her husband when he returned to the hotel. 'Of course,' I answered, 'if it will give him pleasure.' I did, and the next morning about ten, after I sang my second *Walkiria,* the phone rang. It was Maestro Serafin. 'Come at once to my room,' he said. 'But, Maestro, I've not washed yet or dressed; it will take me about half an hour.' 'Never mind, come as you are.'

"Well, you didn't say no to Serafin; we had a real veneration for the maestri then. So, I put on my bathrobe and went down. In his room was the director of the theater. 'Sing the aria you sang for me last night,' Serafin commanded. I did. 'Look, Maria,' he said when I had finished, 'you are going to sing *Puritani* in a week.' 'I can't,' I said. 'I have more *Walkirias;* it's ridiculous—my voice is too heavy.' 'I guarantee you that you can,' Serafin said.

"Well, I thought, if a man like Serafin, who is no child and knows his job, can guarantee this, I would be a fool to say no. So I answered, 'All right, Maestro, but more than my best I cannot promise.' I managed to learn Elvira during my performances of Brünnhilde. I was still young, and being young you have to gamble. But I knew my training was solid, of the good bel canto school, and believe me, bel canto is as essential for Wagner as it is for Bellini. In other words, I had prepared for this challenge. I was ready; there were no surprises.

"In learning any new score, you must approach the music exactly as the composer wrote it. The conductor will give you his cuts, and if there are cadenzas, he will give you ideas about how they should be formed. If he is a conscientious musician, the cadenzas will never be his alone but will be built within the spirit of the music. Bellini is different from Donizetti, and Donizetti is different from Rossini.

"When you have learned the notes, you must then speak the words to yourself to find a natural rhythm. By this, I don't mean how the notes are written—that is set—but, rather, how they must be delivered. This is especially true of recitatives—the introductions to the arias. Recitatives are frequently very attractive in themselves and are always difficult to master, to give a proper rhythm. I learned the value of recitatives at the time of my first Norma, which I prepared with Serafin. After our first rehearsal, he said, 'Now you go home, my dear Miss Callas, and speak these lines to yourself and let's see what proportions, what rhythms you find. Forget that you are singing; forget what is written. Of course, respect what is written, but try to be freer, try to find a flowing rhythm for these recitatives.'

"Singing recitatives is one of many examples of how, in music, you learn to take here and to give back there—the art of rubato, in other words. The main characteristic of Italian music is always a flowing movement, no matter how slowly things go. This is not learned in one day or one week. In fact, I don't think it is ever finished.

"During the period of learning notes—a time of two plus two equals four —you need the help of a good coach who will be hard on you, remind you of each note value and let nothing slip by. It takes a lot of courage to take his advice, because often the greater you become, the less you want to know. But you must brace yourself and say, 'Well, what was wrong?' Sometimes you get very angry—mainly with yourself—and you feel, 'I should have foreseen these things myself.' But often the things you do wrong are the result of bad habits, such as hanging on to words, accenting final syllables too much. You become accustomed to such mistakes and do not hear them, so another must hear them for you.

"Having broken music down into all its parts, you can then take wing. I used to go to every rehearsal, whether I was called or not, so that I could live into the music. And one thing you must do from the first rehearsal is to sing in full voice. This is for your colleagues' sake, for your own sake, to test your possibilities and your strength. Once past the first performance, you can begin real, solid work filling in the missing parts. Prior to this, you have made what is essentially a rough sketch. There is nothing like stage performances before the public to add those details and other intangible things which are so beautiful about music.

"Much of this is combining both movement and music to form a character. I find the meaning for a personage in the music, not in the libretto, though I give enormous attention to words. Still, my dramatic truth comes from the music. As the years go by, a character will deepen if you are a person who likes to grow rather than stand still. For example, my Medea has changed a lot. I saw her first as a very static figure, a barbaric creature who knows what she wants from the beginning. But as I grew, I found Medea a more human figure, though a nasty character. But she was right in her motives; Jason, after all, was even worse than she. So I tried a lot of things to bring out the woman, including a softer hairdo and gestures; I wanted to make her more living, more fascinating.

"My *Traviata* has changed also, though I think my Norma much less so. With Violetta, I gradually realized that her kind of sickness would not permit many or quick movements. I also learned that the less she moves, particularly in the third and fourth acts, the more the music gains. In the last act, so that she would not appear too stiff, I found a number of small, useless gestures. For instance, I had her try to reach her mirror or an item on her dressing table, then drop her hand because there was not enough strength to pick the things up. Also in the last act, I found the breathing had to be short, the color a bit more tired than before. I struggled so hard to find the right quality for this sound. It took a long time to have it, and it was dangerous, like hanging by a thin thread which could break at any moment.

"But we must search and change in order to convince the public of what we are doing, for opera is a dead form in the sense that it is hard today to accept anyone singing 'I love you,' 'I hate you.' This can be spoken, it can be screamed: but it is out of fashion to sing it. Yet we have to ask the public to accept it, and the only way they will is if we bring a bit of fresh air to opera. We must cut certain lengthy music, we must try to bring our movements down to the most believable gestures, we must create an atmosphere in which there is room for understanding. Everything must be as credible as possible within the limitations the composer has left us.

"But often we must be of two minds as well: the performer's mind, which serves the composer, and the public's mind, which listens. We must try and see where a composer might have failed, and how we can help him to reach the audience. Life, after all, is not as it was when the great operas of Verdi and Donizetti were written. People dress differently, they think differently. The only thing that remains the same is deep, honest feelings; I hope it will always be so. But life goes on, and so must opera. We must change with life in order to serve the composer. For this reason, I believe absolutely in cuts.

The repetition of a melody is usually never good. The sooner you come to the point, the better it is. Never risk a second time. There are exceptions, of course. In *Sonnambula* I sang two verses of 'Ah! non giunge,' for it is, frankly, a showpiece, an expression of happiness and joy; pure vocalizing is justified. But when you repeat, you must be careful to vary the music somewhat so that it remains interesting for the public. This is always done, naturally, with good taste and within the style of the composer.

"Conveying all that you have found in a score becomes a sort of drug. If you manage to transmit this to the public, you have a wonderful drunken feeling which becomes contagious all around. Still, once you have finished a day or a performance, you must look at yourself and say, 'Well, this or that happened.' You forget the good things and try to discover how you can improve the bad ones. Perhaps I am too analytical, but I prefer that to simply sitting back and resting on my glory. That is the end of great art. When you are happy with what you have done, there is no progress. It is a matter of pride, I suppose, to feel that you have done your best, but it also makes you strive to do more.

"My biggest problem is that I am a terrible pessimist. I often think I am incapable of doing well, so I always try to do better. But there is the danger of trying too hard and ruining something beautiful by losing control or exaggerating. But a good, hard, sensible look at your work is still the best teacher an artist can have.

"But so few, I find, do this. Today, there are not many who are really ready to sing. I don't mean there are not beautiful voices; but there are few beautiful voices with a schooling good enough to undertake major roles. Singers need experience, and you cannot have the proper experience by beginning at the Metropolitan Opera or La Scala. Experience is obtained by starting in small theaters and coming up the hard way. This is not something people like to do. But if you do, by the time you reach the big houses you will be fully equipped for the challenge. There is no space for amateurs.

"In my opinion, opera is the most difficult of all the arts. To succeed, you must not only be a first-rate musician but a first-rate actor. It goes without saying that you must also be able to cope with your colleagues—first with the conductor, then with the other singers, with the stage director—for opera is a vast unit where everyone plays a vital role.

"I accepted the classes at Juilliard in order to help singers start off on the right foot. Of course, the trouble for some young singers is that they accept engagements before they are ready, and once they've experienced being on an operatic stage, it's very difficult for them to come back and study. Humility is not one of our best traits. I would like to pass on to the young ones what I have learned from great conductors, from my teachers, and especially from my own research, which has not stopped to this day. I suppose I have a natural insight into music, but I take the trouble to see what lies beneath a composer's work. We must never forget that we are interpreters, that we are there to serve the composer and to discharge a very delicate task.

"Also, great stages with great traditions ought to be respected. You must know your way around; part of this is not using your vocal capital, only the interest. If you serve art well, everything will come automatically: you will be great, you will have money, there will be fame. But the work is hard, in the beginning, during, and afterwards.

"But it is a privilege. I consider myself privileged because I have been able to bring truth from the soul and the mind, give it to the public, and have it accepted. Not everyone can do that. It is one of the greatest powers one can put at the service of one of the greatest arts—music."

THE CLASSES

MOZART ❧ DON GIOVANNI

ACT II: *"Non mi dir"*

"Mozart is usually sung with too much delicacy, as though the singer were on tiptoes, when his music should be performed with the same frankness and bel canto approach one would use in *Il trovatore,* for example. Mozart, after all, was a master of bel canto, and a necessity of bel canto is a full, sustained tone and good legato. So sing Mozart as though he were Verdi; there is no difference in the approach.

"In the recitative before this aria, I would not fill in the interval of a third on 'Crudele?' as is traditional:

Cru - de - le?

Remember, there must always be a reason for an embellishment, or don't use one. Here, Donna Anna is shocked that her lover, Don Ottavio, has called her 'cruel.' She repeats the word as though to accuse him in return. The phrase is strong as it stands; with the usual passing tone, it becomes too soft, too sweet. Later, however, I would insert an upward appoggiatura on the word 'desìa,' to give it more color when Anna speaks of what 'our soul desires,' and I would use the passing tone with 'Ma il mondo,' because it needs to contrast with the outcry 'O Dio!' which follows:

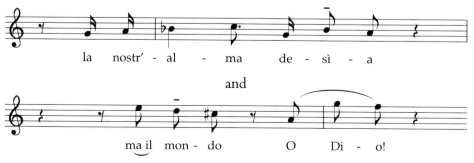

la nostr' - al - ma de - sì - a

and

ma il mon - do   O Di - o!

"As you emphasize 'O Dio!' to set it off from 'ma il mondo,' and because it is from her heart, you must first weigh well 'Ah no, mio bene!' following 'Crudele?'; this is Anna's defense of herself:

"In the second part of this recitative—'Troppo mi spiace'—you can begin after the orchestral chord rather than with it, as written. This will give the line more breadth and your entry more repose. Do not, however, become tense here; the words must not be rushed—they must flow. Keep the whole mood relaxed once past 'Crudele?' and your colors not too dark.

"Be careful when you come to 'abbastanza per te':

"Do not sing 'ab/ba/stan/za,' but make one legato line to the B-flat and away from it, and do not sing the B-flat too piano. This is classical music, yes, but it must have its vibrancy.

"Begin the larghetto with a good, clean attack on 'Non' and follow it with a firm, strong line. Anna, after all, is reassuring Ottavio of her love, so be affirmative, let it breathe, don't tighten up:

"Next come three phrases beginning with the word 'tu.' With each, lean heavily on the vowel; make it a good *oo* sound. In the second phrase—'tu conosci la mia fè'—again be careful not to separate too much. Do not sing 'tu/co/no/sci' but tie the notes together with a good legato. Keep to the line:

"The next is a small matter, but it is attention to details that makes a performance. In 'calma il tuo tormento,' distinguish between the pair of thirty-second notes and the sixteenths that follow:

"After the first 'non vuoi ch'io mora'—and be careful throughout to put the *ch* on 'ch'io'; this could escape you—take a deep breath before the repeat of the phrase and try to carry your phrase over into the return of 'Non mi dir.' It can be sung with a break after the fermata on 'mora,' but to me it is less stylish and causes the music to stop its flow:

"Also, watch the pronunciation of 'mora' at the cadence. Stress the *o* and add the *r* at the very last moment. If you add the *r* too soon, your voice could close up and spoil the climax. Later, I would take a breath after the A-flat on 'vuoi' before the allegretto begins. It will not only give the line more interest but will allow you to make a more sustained phrase on the 'ch'io mora' which leads into the allegretto:

"In the allegretto, actually the aria's cabaletta, be careful, with the many two-note phrases and the vocalises on 'ah,' not to alter your vocal color. Keep your voice in the same position and with one sound throughout:

ah_____

And, on the third 'pietà,' I would phrase it two by two. It lends the line more character:

(pie) -tà,_____

"Also, at the very end, I would sing the final flourish on 'ah' rather than 'pietà' as written. Try it both ways to see what suits your voice best, but to me 'ah' is easier. Whichever you choose, do not sing the notes down from A on 'di,' as in the score; the phrase will become too choppy: 'di-i-i-i.' Instead, use 'pietà di':

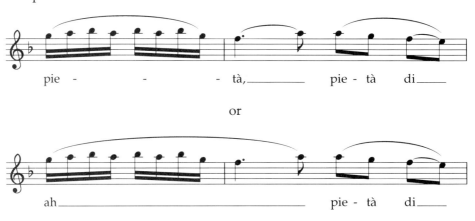

pie - - - tà,_____ pie - tà di_____

or

ah_____ pie - tà di_____

MOZART ☙ *COSÌ FAN TUTTE*

ACT I: *"Come scoglio"*

"In this decisive, bold piece of writing, Fiordiligi is ordering a would-be suitor from her home: 'How dare you; get out of here. Do not profane this house with your treacherous words.' This music must be well underlined with your voice, especially with your chest voice. Without good low notes here, properly placed, the bottom of the aria will fall out. Sing it with an open throat, and keep the music always moving forward, but with good accents, especially in the opening recitative. It is not easy to emphasize words well and keep the line alive; but, then, has anyone ever told you that singing was easy? It is 'Te-me-RA-ri,' 'FUO-ri,' 'LO-co':

"I would sing the second phrase, 'e non profani l'alito infausto degl'infami detti,' in one breath, eliminating the written rest:

"The first change in mood comes with 'ai cari amanti.' Here, Fiordiligi vows to remain faithful to her true love. Make this phrase tender, molto legato:

"You will notice that most of the phrases in this recitative end with two eighth notes. Be careful not to exaggerate these, as in 'morte.' Give them only their written value:

"The aria itself must be authoritative, even, secure. Sing in the middle of the notes:

In the wide skips that occur throughout, keep your pitches clean and attack the note in the face—no scooping. Remember, full low notes:

con - tra i ven - ti,   e   la

"Attack the trill on G right on the principal note. If you have a doubt as to where to begin a trill, it is on the note written. If the composer wants the trill to begin from above, he will give you an appoggiatura to the main note. Always presume, as well, it is a whole-tone trill unless the composer specifically indicates a half-tone. Remember, too, a trill is always written for an expressive reason. For example, the trills in 'D'amor sull'ali rosee' from the last act of *Trovatore* represent fear. In this *Così* aria, the trill reinforces the strength of Fiordiligi's love. The emotion of the particular moment will tell you if the trill is fast or slow and how it is to be colored:

can - gi af - fet - - - to   il   cor,

"In the next phrase, I would eliminate 'affetti' so that you can sing the vocalise to high C on 'ah.' Keep your vocalizing here legato, no separations:

can - gi,   ah_____

"The last section of the aria, più allegro, must be very secco, and again the triplets should be sung on 'ah.' They must be very even, very legato. Watch the direction of these triplets; point them downward so that the low notes will not be lost:

spe - ra (ah)_____

"The approach to the last two B-flats is difficult. If you find yourself in trouble, you might take a breath just before B-flat. This, of course, is not correct, but a breath is better than ruining the phrase:

non vi ren - - - da au - da - (ci)

Better still, change the words like this if you need the breath:

non vi ren - da au - da - (ci)

MOZART ᴂ *DIE ZAUBERFLÖTE*

ACT I: *"O zitt're nicht"*

"This aria must be commanding in order to convey the grave importance of the Queen of the Night. You must not feel separate notes here; tie one tone to another. Furthermore, the aria must be sung with strong low notes as well. I have recordings by Lilli Lehmann, who sang both the Queen of the Night and Norma in the last century. Believe me, she had her low tones, her chest notes. You must have them and *use* them to convey the great authority of the Queen. Remember that in neither of her arias has Mozart written a piano, and I feel the necessity for a compelling sound in both.

"It is not enough to have a high D or F in this music. These notes, of course, are very nice, but they are not the main thing; either you have them or you don't. What is of more importance is the great strength of this woman, and this you will capture only with a well-supported, sustained sound. From the very first phrase, give the notes their full value:

O zitt - re nicht, mein lie - ber Sohn!

At the end of the recitative do not let your voice drop when the line drops, but keep it full:

ACT I:
"O zitt're nicht"

Mut - ter - herz   zu   tröst - en.

"Perhaps you will feel the beginning of the aria as piano. If so, never let it be a childish sound. Authority does not mean that you must always sing forte, but it does mean that you must take full measure of the words. However you begin the aria, it must be a good cantabile:

Zum   Lei - den   bin   ich   au - ser - ko - ren,

"Watch phrases such as:

Ach_____ helft!   Ach_____ helft!

There is a danger of letting out too much breath on them. Vowels must always dominate your diction, even in German; the purer the vowel, the more supported the rest of the voice remains. I am afraid German is sung much too harshly today. Of course, we want clear diction; we must have it. But it must not be overdone. Often phrases sag because time has been wasted attempting to attack a German word and to put an ending on it. Be easy with accents in German; make them with tone and not breath.

"Also, treat ornaments in Mozart as you would those in Bellini—on the beat, well oiled and directly stated:

Hül - - - fe

and

ge - hen,

"The opening of the allegro—

—must also have authority, but you do not need to push your voice to achieve this. Do it with tone, attack, and support. When you reach the gruppetti, start them immediately; don't lose time and momentum:

Do your vocalizing on 'ah,' not 'ha'—no aspirates, ever!

"In studying such phrases, I would break them down into groups of four or even eight notes and go at them like a machine, with good hard accents on the first of each group. Hammer them out as a pianist would until they are set in your throat. Be aware of every pitch as you work, especially the differences between the half and whole tones, which are tricky here. At all times keep your support; never let these scales and turns sound sick.

"When you reach the trill, make your attack right on the note as written; there is no time to begin slowly and then increase the speed. It must be an instant trill:

"Finally, do not let down after the scales and the top F are over; the aria must come to a full conclusion if you are to convince the public you *are* the

Queen of the Night. Actually, this conclusion is more important than the vocalization that has gone before it, for it is a summing up:

ACT II: *"Der Hölle Rache"*

"With any aria, and especially this one, you must show an audience what you are going to give them before you begin singing. In other words, it would be wrong to begin this great vengeance aria with a smile on your face. Even more than the first aria for the Queen of the Night, this one requires authority. She is furious here, and you must reflect this before you have sung a note.

"I hear this piece as very secco throughout, extremely rhythmic and full in tone from the first phrase:

"Again, there are diction problems here which will impede you if you let them, words such as:

It is impossible to give each of these a beginning and an end while maintaining the drive of the aria. Some compromise is necessary; personally, I would lean heavily on the vowels to keep the line moving.

"On a bigger scale, remember each aria or scene has its beginning and an end; in between there are many little arches, all of which must be carefully planned. You must always know just where you are heading, where a phrase will end and just how much breath it will take. Never leave any of this to chance.

"When you reach the famous staccati, make certain you do not lose the acciaccatura at the beginning. Keep the staccati crystalline, like glass; there must be a ping to the sound. Above all, *no* crescendi; they must all be the same:

ah

"Once again, be especially conscious of the final phrase after the staccati:

so   bist   du   mei - ne   Toch - ter

This is once more a summing up and mustn't be slighted.

"Later, with the repeated F's, which are almost like fanfares, be certain you keep your tone full. Do not peck at these notes; they are too important:

Ver - stos - sen   sei   auf   e - wig

"The most difficult part of this aria is not the staccati to high F; it is the triplets that will make you sweat blood. Groups of three are the most difficult thing in all of singing to vocalize evenly:

ah

Attack them right in the face, no slow start, and don't let yourself drop behind the tempo. If you slacken the tempo, it makes singing more difficult than necessary. Think quickly here, and again watch carefully the differences between half and whole steps.

"While we must always strive to perform like an instrumentalist, the voice is not an instrument and gets tired. Therefore, in order to save it, we often have to practice mentally. For example, these triplets could be studied while sitting quietly in your room. Go over and over them with your mind. Think the notes, but do no more than hum them. Eventually, you will have them in your head and know where you are going without unduly using your voice.

"I don't know if a conductor would permit it or not, but I would make an accelerando towards the end of the next set of staccati; it makes a more dramatic effect and enables you to sing all four measures in a single breath:

ah _____

"Again, sing with good strength and support the phrase after the staccati:

wenn nicht   durch dich   Sa - ra - stro wird er - (blassen!)

Make the final note before the fermata short for dramatic impact:

blas - sen!

"With the final notes—

Hört,   hört,   hört, _____

—be very aware of what you are saying: 'Listen, listen, gods of vengeance,' and really let your voice out. Again, watch a word like 'hört.' Do not expend too much air on the *h;* the vowel is much more important. Take good advantage of the fermata before the first 'hört.' Use it for a dramatic pause and for a good, deep breath. Then, attack 'hört' like a bolt of lightning. Here, more than at any other point in the aria, she is the commanding queen, and you must invest her with all the power and darkness she deserves.

ACT II: *"Ach, ich fühl's"*

"Dramatically this aria is a simple, direct statement of Pamina's state of mind at this particular moment. Yet it must have expression. In Mozart, as in Bellini, anguish is anguish, and the public must be made to feel it. But too many singers lose expression in Mozart because they overdo the pianos, overdo the style. They do Mozart an injustice. His music is not frilly lace; it is music to be felt as deeply as any other.

"Though this aria is marked andante, it must always flow. Be especially careful when you reach the vocalises on 'Herzen':

Her -   -   -   -   - (zen)

If you slow these down, you will harm the effect the phrase can have and make the music sound too precious. Also, sing the low notes, particularly the C-sharp in 'im Tode sein,' with a full sound:

so   wird   Ruh'_____   im   To -   - de   sein,

Pamina is saying she will find peace only in death. This is a strong idea, and it must be reinforced by your voice."

BEETHOVEN ⊗ *"AH! PERFIDO"*

"Though not from an opera, 'Ah! perfido' deals with strong feelings. A woman deserted by her lover cries out to heaven to punish him, then begs the gods to take her life instead. In short, she does not know her own mind. Beethoven reflects this in many changes of tempo and mood as the character expresses one emotion one moment and another the next. The difficulty here is to capture these moods yet keep a sense of the whole.

"Begin very forcefully, using the A of 'Ah!' and the A of 'spergiuro' as springboards to the next notes. It should be 'Ah! PER-fi-do, sper-GIU-ro'—'perfidious one, false one':

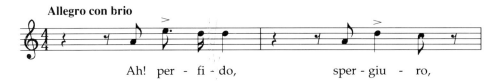

"Tie the words closely to the notes with a well-supported sound. This scene is written in so many sections that unless you keep it moving ahead steadily with a good legato, it will fall apart.

"After this bitter opening comes the first change of mood—'e son questi gl'ultimi tuoi congedi?' [and this is your last farewell?]:

"Begin this phrase after the orchestral chord. In fact, think of the andante which follows as coming a measure earlier. This will open the phrase up, give it a feeling of relaxation and emphasize the change of mood. This line must have a good shape—point it towards the F of 'tuoi'—as must the phrase that follows, 'Ove s'intese tirannìa più crudel.' Both must be kept moving once you have begun them, and both must be sung with authority even though they are piano. Just because you are singing piano does not mean that there can be no authority; you must create it with words rather than tone. Also, in 'Ove s'intese,' watch your note values carefully, do not lose details, such as the '-a' in 'tirannìa,' and head the line to 'più'—'Where has one found tyranny *more* cruel?':

O - ve s'in-te - se ti - ran - ni - a più cru - del?

"Here and throughout the scene, remember that even when you slow down you must always keep a regular pulsation going; everything must be measured in your mind and in your voice. When you reach 'Va, scellerato,' again think of the tempo change, allegro assai, as coming a measure earlier. This way your voice will lead the music into its next mood:

Va, scel - le - ra - to! va, pur fug - gi da me,

Let's have a good accent on 'FUG-gi,' and don't forget to pronounce clearly both *g*'s—'fug-gi.'

"A few measures later we have yet another mood, andante grave. Begin it—'Se v'è giustizia in ciel'—with weight in your voice, but be rhythmically correct, full note values, and do not let it drag:

Se v'è giu - sti - zia in ciel,

"At the climax—'vedrò le mie vendette' [I will see my vengeance]—attack the A's straight on, immediately:

ve - drò le mie ven - det - te;

"The next line, allegro assai, must also be as direct. This is one of the spots where the scene could begin to falter if you are not careful. You will need a breath after 'immaginando,' but make it a quick one so that you continue moving towards the allegro con brio which comes next:

io   già le go-do im-ma-gi- nan-do;   i ful-mi-ni ti

Allegro con brio

veg - go   già ba - le - nar d'in - tor - no.

"We must again open the music up at 'Ah no! ah no!' by transferring the adagio of the next bar forward a measure:

Adagio

Ah, no!____   ah, no!____   fer - ma - te,

This is necessary because the opening drama is over. We now have the more classic side of the music, as the woman changes her mind—'risparmiate quel cor, ferite il mio!' [spare that heart, strike mine!]:

ri - spar - mia - te quel cor, fe - ri - te il mi - o!

"The final part of this opening scene is very sustained and softer, but not delicate; there still must be body to the sound as she says 's'ei non è più qual era, son io qual fui' [if he is no more as he was, I am as I was]. Highlight 'era' [was] and 'io' [I]:

s'ei non è più qual e - ra,   son' io qual fu - i;

"Also, on 'per lui vivea' [for him I lived] go straight to the E-flat—don't linger on the F—and make the last phrase—'voglio morir per lui' [I want to die for him]—rich in feeling, emphasizing the F-sharp of 'morir' and the G of 'per':

per lui vi - ve - a,   vog - lio mo - rir   per lu - i!

"With the conclusion of the opening scene, the most difficult part of the aria is behind you, provided you can sing it with a good, long line. It must be calm, tender, and very sustained. At the beginning, keep your voice somewhat confined; don't let it out too much. Watch your vowels: a round *ah* at the end of 'pietà,' and a good *e* sound in 'addio.' Be careful, too, to keep the line clean. There will be a tendency to slide up from the first 'pietà' to 'non dirmi addio.' Instead, keep the pitches firm and attack 'non' on the note:

Per pie - tà, non dir— mi ad - di - o,

"Later, watch the *o* of 'farò.' Don't let it become too covered—it is *o*, not *oo:*

pri - va che— fa - rò?———

"Remember, on 'Tu lo sai'—and this is true back at 'Ah no! ah no!' as well—that the small note is not an acciaccatura but an appoggiatura which gets half of the value of the note it precedes:

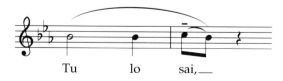

Tu   lo   sai,—

We have already seen this in the *Don Giovanni* aria as well; it is a common notation from before Mozart through Verdi.

"You must vibrate the next phrase, 'bell' idol mio.' It is the first time she speaks of the man with love, and the phrase says she still loves him very much:

bell'_____ i - dol_ mi - o,

"At the first cadence, I would carry the B-flat of 'morirò' down to G, then take a breath before beginning 'Per pietà.' This will make the return of the main theme more expressive:

mo - ri - rò._____   Per pie - (tà)

"The second statement of the aria is in the same sustained mood as the first until you reach 'Io d'affanno,' rising to G-flat. This needs power, because it is a summing up and takes us into the coda:

io d'af - fan - no___

Against the pizzicati in the orchestra, make the next 'io d'affanno' like a sigh:

io   d'af - fan - no

And on the arpeggio keep the line clean and the pitches true:

i -   o_____ d'af - (fanno)

The low B-flats should be full:

mo -   ri - rò,

At the cadence, make the B-natural and C precise in pitch, and crescendo on them:

mo - ri - rò.

"The allegro assai must be a fury, a storm. Be sure to accent 'Ah' well or it will be lost:

Ah cru - del! cru - del! tu vuoi

"When the più lento comes, 'Dite voi, se in tanto affanno,' keep it moving; do not let the two-note phrases lag:

Di - te voi, se in tan - to af - fan - no

non— son— de - gna di— pie - tà,—

"The finale begins with the next allegro assai. Attack the A-flat in the face as well as the B-flat of the next phrase:

Ah! cru - del,— tu— vuoi— ch'io— mo - ra!

Keep the music alive and moving through to the più lento. Breathe well before the last high A-flat ('sì barbara') and do not let the two-note phrases that follow drag:

bar - ba - ra, si bar - ba - ra— mer - cè?

"When you reach the chromatic scales in the next allegro assai, keep them clean and light. If you slow down here, you are lost:

ah

"With the exception of a few bars of adagio, which must be very, very calm before the last outburst, the problem now is to sustain through the heroics of the final pages. You can do this if you take good, deep breaths after each 'pietà' so that you are ready for the many B-flats Beethoven has written. They are very exciting for an audience but very draining on a singer.

BEETHOVEN ✌ *FIDELIO*

ACT I: *"Abscheulicher!"*

"This aria is the outburst of a woman who has suffered enormously and has dedicated her life to freeing her husband from prison. This fact will affect everything you do with her music. For example, Leonora's piano cannot be a delicate one; it must be full. And though the aria itself is very romantic, it must have tension, a sense of concentrated power, so that the decisive section, allegro con brio, comes as a natural consequence of her inner thoughts. In other words, you must always be a heroine.

"Be very conscious throughout of vowels. The words are difficult and can trip you up if you do not handle them with care. Be in control every moment; know what you are doing and where you are going.

"Leonora's first cry, 'Abscheulicher!' [Monster!] must come as the climax of the orchestra's agitato beginning. Make it forward and pointed in sound:

Ab - scheu - li - cher!   wo eilst du hin?

Keep her thoughts moving straight through 'in wildem Grimme' without letting your drive up.

"The first change in mood comes with 'Des Mitleids Ruf.' Here the sound should be more relaxed and warm:

She is asking if 'the call of pity, the voice of humanity' cannot stir Pizarro, the monster who has imprisoned her Florestan. Take a breath after 'rührt nichts' so that you can emphasize well 'mehr deinen Tigersinn.' This should have almost a snarl to it. The 'tiger's mind' is Pizarro's:

"With the next allegro, sing right on the *o* of 'Doch' or it will slow you down:

And when she says 'in me there shines a rainbow,' make it very expressive, but always within a classic framework; this is not Puccini!

"Finally, sing the poco sostenuto with strong rhythm. This must be strictly in time or it could break down and spoil all you have built so far:

"The aria, adagio, is a study in legato. Keep it calm and well measured, especially in the scale passages. When you reach 'O komm, erhell',' make it very expressive, with a full sound on 'O komm.' And *try* to sing the phrase that follows in one breath:

"It will be too much to try the phrase up to high B and down in one breath. I would finish 'erreichen' on the D-sharp, breathe, and repeat the word to finish the phrase:

"Afterwards, give great feeling to 'Hoffnung'—hope. This is the main idea in Leonora's mind:

"Like 'Doch' in the recitative, watch 'noch' at the end of the aria. Do not lose time and breath on it. Keep to the vowel:

Make no ritard on the last three notes of the aria, but sing them strongly to push yourself into the allegro con brio finale:

(er) - rei - - - chen.

"The allegro must be secco from the beginning but firm. It moves without letup until you reach 'und süssen Trost dir bringen!' 'I bring you sweet comfort,' Leonora sings to Florestan, and you must emphasize this well. Beethoven has instructed the orchestra to wait for the singer here, so make the most of it before the allegro returns:

und süs - sen Trost dir brin - gen!
(colla parte)

"Once the allegro starts again, it goes relentlessly to the finish. One point: I would break the phrase on 'Gatten,' which drops to a low B-sharp. Finish the word on the upper C-sharp, breathe well and continue on *ah*, finishing on 'die Liebe.' This gives the phrase more drive and makes it more exciting:

Gat - - - ten ah_____ die lie - be,

"Make the repeated G-sharps like a trumpet call:

nein, nein, ich wan - ke nicht,

On the last G-sharp, held for two measures, gradually crescendo and then breathe before the final scale. If you prefer, these scales can be sung on *ah* instead of 'Gatten.' If you choose *ah*, then end the phrase on 'die Liebe':

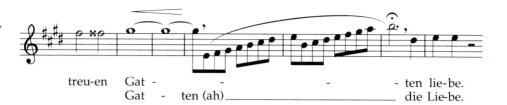

"Incidentally, some singers add an appoggiatura upward to F-sharp before the final note. To my mind, it is cleaner and more dramatic to sing the end as written."

CHERUBINI ✑ MEDEA
ACT I: "Dei tuoi figli"

"This aria is a killer. It is difficult at the beginning and more difficult at the end. Before you try to sing it, plan it out carefully, cold-bloodedly; find where its problems are and how you can solve them. In particular, get the rhythm down precisely; work on it just as you would a difficult passage in a piano piece, with slow, meticulous study. Do not try to add exterior passion until you are confident with the aria's internal demands. In opera, passion without intellect is no good; you will be a wild animal and not an artist.

"Look at this music and say to yourself, 'I have not only to go from the beginning of this aria here to the ending there, but I have a duet to sing afterwards as well as two more acts, which are also killers. How will I do this?' First, remember that while Medea is a hard woman, she is also a woman in love. This aria is her first and last chance in the opera to be kind and loving. Even though she accuses Jason, she wants him back. Take advantage of the loving side of Medea; use phrases such as 'torna a me, torna sposo per me' [come back to me, come back to me as my husband] to relax, to spare yourself and your voice for the cries of 'crudel' and those B-flats towards the end. If you sing the whole aria as big as its climaxes, you are dead.

"Remember, too, this is a classical piece. The approach to *Medea* is the same as that to *Don Giovanni, Fidelio,* or *Vestale:* precise pitches, clean rhythm, a strong line.

"Begin the larghetto calmly and in a steady pace. Watch the pair of sixteenth notes in the first phrase; they must not be rushed and they must be accurate in pitch. Also, get off the G of 'madre,' not only so that the line will continue to move but so that you take a good breath for the next phrase. And it is 'Dei TUOI figli,' not 'Dei tuoi FI-gli':

Dei tuoi fi - gli la__ ma - dre

"In the next two phrases, be careful to pronounce the double consonants in 'afflitta' and 'fatta':

vin - ta e af - flit - ta,   fat - ta

"With 'crudel,' and each repetition of it (and there are many), attack both notes well and secco:

cru - del   and   cru - del!

Be careful here and in the line down from A ('a te fu cara') not to vibrate your sound too much or you will be overworked early in the game. If anything, Medea's drama should be on the lean rather than the fat side. Keep your throat open at all times, and control the music with breath, not with tone. Also, do not scoop on 'crudel'; you'll kill yourself:

cru - del   a____ te____ fu____ ca - ra ____

"Twice Medea sings 'scacciata, dolorosa' [driven out, sad]. Here, as in 'torna a me,' you can make the drama work for you. The first phrase, 'scacciata,' must be accented and hard, but 'dolorosa' can be softer, more espressivo. It is, after all, said almost in self-pity:

scac - cia - ta,   do - lo - ro - sa,   scac - cia - ta,   do - lo - ro - sa,

"Watch the phrase beginning 'se mai mi fossi.' Keep it clean. Sing it with ease but be absolutely rhythmical:

se   mai____   mi__   fos - si   ap - par - so

"At the end of the phrase, with the first B-flat, take advantage of the fermata to breathe deeply and to clear the air of the preceding tension, for the next phrase has to be very inward and calm:

le or - ren - de pas-sio - - ni;   scor - re - a la__

"Again, take care with sixteenth notes, this time on 'sereno':

se - - - re - - - no

"Medea has a big outcry at 'ho dato tutto a te' [I have given you every-thing], which must be balanced immediately with expressiveness in 'torna sposo per me':

ho da - to tut-to a   te: tor - na spo - so per me!

"After the next two 'crudel's—remember, clean attacks!—wait and breathe well before beginning 'Io non voglio':

cru - del!   cru - del!   Io non vo - glio che__

"In some performances of *Medea* you will find the repeat of 'non voglio che te solo' omitted—about a measure of music. Why, I do not know.

I have sung it both ways. In my first recording with Maestro Serafin, we omitted it, and I sang the notes for 'solo' to the words 'sol te.' Two years later, he reinstated this missing bar:

"When you reach the 'pietà's, breathe well before and after each. This will not only give the thought emphasis but will prepare you for the B-flats, especially the difficult ones in 'per tanto amor':

"And each 'torna a me' will be hushed to contrast with the 'pietà's:

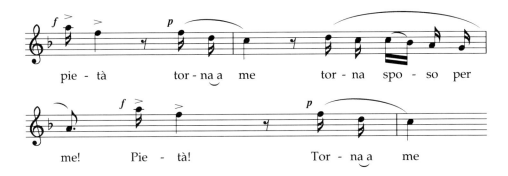

"The exceptions, of course, are the final two statements of 'torna sposo per me,' which ride up to B-flat. You have no choice but to sing these out. But prepare them with deep breaths. Believe me, you will need all the help you can get here:

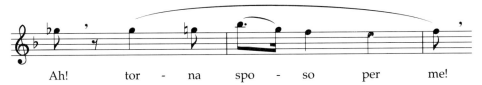

"The return of the aria's first theme in the orchestra before the last 'pietà' is always omitted so that this cry will have its full effect. Perform the ending like this:

cor!   Pie - tà!

SPONTINI ❧ *LA VESTALE*

ACT II: *"Tu che invoco"*

"This difficult aria is very heavy and should only be sung by a dramatic voice. Still, it is an excellent study for any soprano for diction, line, and sustaining tone.

"Do not sing the first part too slowly. It will help your breathing if you keep it moving; if you animate the music, all of its difficulties will be easier. Make a firm attack on the first note, a good *oo* sound. I prefer the first phrase to go through 'orrore,' but breathe if you must after 'invoco.' This section lies right in the passaggio of the soprano voice, and it might be difficult for you to sustain the line without help. Don't forget to roll the double *r*'s of 'orrore' and to make your acciaccature expressive. Be careful to make a distinction between the acciaccature of the aria and the appoggiature which come later, after the aria:

"At 'alfin m'ascolta' sing 'al-' on F instead of the preceding E-flat. Often we must rearrange words if they are awkward and if the line can be strengthened by the change:

"Take a good breath before beginning the long phrase on 'questo misero mio core.' Remember: when you feel yourself running out of breath in such a phrase, do not slow down; you will only strangle. If anything, press the line forward. Also, I would sing the descending scale from F on 'che' and eliminate 'fa.' It makes it easier to round off the scale before 'possa respirar':

Again, when you reach 'i miei contrasti,' move 'i' to the second F, like this:

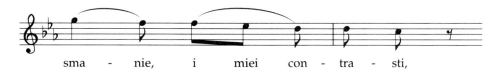

"Gradually build the animando which follows until you are hammering out the G's and the A-flats. The breathing is tricky here. I prefer 'in me l'ardore' in one breath, but you can break before '-re' if absolutely necessary. Do not observe the fermata on E-flat as you come down to 'dissipar':

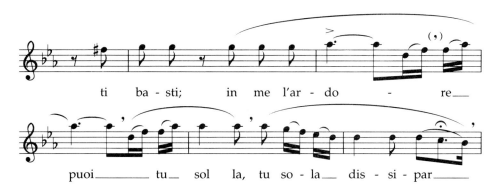

"Another necessary change in the words comes on the second 'puoi tu.' Here and a few measures later, simply exchange the two words:

"Usually the first eight bars of the aria's postlude are cut and only the final five before the presto are performed:

so - la dis - si - par.

"The recitative that follows is placed badly for a soprano, but you must strive to give it importance. The orchestra here will remain very rhythmic in its outbursts, but in between you can be free. Take the time to pronounce well. This is, after all, recitativo, and liberties are necessary to bring it to life.

"Watch carefully the appoggiature here. Sing both notes in the case of a long appoggiatura—

la   sa - cri - - - le - ga   ma - no.

—but only the appoggiatura in the case of a short one:

L'o - dio - so a - spet - to   mi - o

"When you reach 'immortal fiamma,' invert these two words; the original does not fit the voice well:

quest fiam - ma im - mor - tal

"Really let out your sound at 'Amore, tu il vuoi, m'arrendo.' It will be easier on you and more dramatic to make this moment big. Breathe well before 'm'arrendo,' and accent these notes well, secco:

A - mo - re, tu il_ vuo - i, tu il vuo - i, m'ar-ren-do...

"It is very important in the prestissimo to keep the rhythm strict and sing on the words:

Ma do - ve io por - to il piè?..

I would work the text out slowly without singing; speak it until it flows naturally.

"Do not let up your drive until you reach the lento. Here we have a complete change in mood as Giulia speaks her lover's name ('Ma Licinio'). It must be sung with a caress; you must make the public know this is a name she loves. However, wait until the orchestra dies away before beginning this new mood. The orchestra has made a lot of sound, and it will take a moment for the public to absorb it and be ready to receive your sound:

Ma Li - ci - nio

"Just before the molto agitato, I would again let the orchestra finish before singing 'No.' Pause, take a good breath, then 'no, non' is in tempo:

"Let's have a good *oo* on 'più,' and ignore the rest after 'delitto.' You don't need a breath here, and the line will be stronger:

"The final section, presto assai, must be strong, well weighted, and carefully measured. The drive does not stop; it is like Medea's music. You have a cut here, however, which helps, from page 135 (Ricordi) to the bottom of 136:

"The most difficult part of the finale is once more a question of diction. 'Poi sommessa alla vostra possanza quella vita fatal che m'avanza.' The words must be clear, but well within your sound. Until you can speak this text in

your sleep, the aria will never be convincing. Work on the words slowly
without singing until they are set in your mind. You must be precise in your
pitches as well:

Poi som - mes_ sa al - la vo - stra pos - san - za

quel - la vi - ta fa - tal_ che m'a - van - za

"At the very end, 'del vostro furor,' do not make a rallentando, and
emphasize the words with good accents:

sia l'og - get - to del vo - stro fu - ror.

ROSSINI ✤ *IL BARBIERE DI SIVIGLIA*

ACT II: *"Una voce poco fa"*

"Rosina is a determined young Spanish girl. She is very sure of herself and accustomed to having her way; there is nothing precious about her. Later in the opera she is almost coy when she wants something, but not here. These are private thoughts. She has just heard a voice that pleases her—Almaviva's serenade in the first act—and she is still thinking about it. So sweeten up the beginning of the aria; it must have a smile in it. Open up your throat:

"The phrase must also move; don't let the rhythm slacken. When she says Lindoro's name the first time—remember, Almaviva is Lindoro to Rosina—it must be with love. Caress the phrase:

"Don't lose the acciaccature on 'Lindoro mio sarà':

Sì, Lin - do - - - ro___ mio___ sa - rà,

"Here and in 'la vincerò' keep the line moving. Observe the rests that are written, but give them their value and no more. The B of 'la vincerò' needs chest voice to underscore her thoughts—'I will triumph, Lindoro will be mine':

lo___ giu - ra - i, la___ vin - ce - rò,

"There are those who are afraid of chest voice and say if you sing in the chest, you will have no high notes. Yet I made my career on both. You *must* have both for the sake of expression. Again, if you listen to old recordings, you will find that even light sopranos in the last century had their chest notes. But the notes were well placed within the voice. This is the secret.

"Incidentally, many singers attempt to avoid the low notes of this aria by transposing it to the key of F. To my mind, this is wrong. It gives the aria an entirely different attitude.

"On the second 'Sì, Lindoro mio sarà,' attack the G-sharp lightly and sing the downward scales in tempo. The same is true of 'lo giurai,' though I would emphasize the C-sharp of 'giurai.' Do not roll the *r*'s here. As a general rule, you roll in Italian only when there is a double *r*. Also, this word begins not *gee-oo*, but is like the English word 'Jew,' short; in other words, one syllable, not two. End with a good *ee* sound on 'giurai':

sì, Lin - do - ro___ mio___ sa -
- rà, lo giu - - ra - i,

"In the next section we learn of Rosina's stronger side. 'My tutor will soon come home,' she tells us, 'and I will outsmart him. He will object, but Lindoro will be mine.' The words are very clear here; you do not need to overdo them for the public. Just be playful, confident, not cute. Put the words as much in your face and eyes as in your voice:

Il tu-tor ri-cu-se - rà,   io l'in-ge-gno a-guz-ze - rò,

"It is traditional to alter passages in this aria and in many bel canto works. I recommend that you obtain Luigi Ricci's book of cadenzas and ornaments published by Ricordi. It will be of help to you. For example, the standard change for 'alla fin s'accheterà' is given by Ricci:

al - la fin s'ac-che-te - rà   e con - ten - ta io re - ste - rò.

"A pair of cadenzas are also traditional for the end of the first half of the aria after 'e contenta io resterò.' These are mine:

Sì, Lin-do - - - ro mio sa-rà, lo_giu-

- ra - i, la vin-ce-ro sì, Lin-do - - ro____

mi - o_sa - rà, lo_____ giu - ra - i,

ah____

ah_____   Ah!   sì.

"One word of caution; whichever cadenzas you use, keep them simple and in the right spirit. Rossini once heard a famous artist sing this *Barbiere* aria, and when she had finished, he said, 'Beautiful, beautiful, but tell me—who wrote the music?' She had so overdecorated the piece that Rossini pretended not to recognize it. He disapproved of heavy ornamentation, and I must say, so do I. Believe me, you will make a better effect with good feeling in your voice than with the hullabaloo of a lot of notes. Of course, people will say, 'Oh! What a wonderful display.' But so what? Are you after fireworks or expression?

"We learn even more about Rosina in the second half of the aria. 'I am docile,' she says at the beginning, 'respectful, obedient.' However, later she adds, '*But*— if you cross me, I will become a viper.' So the opening must have some irony to it, because we know what is to come. Part of the irony can be conveyed by the acciaccature Rossini has given you on 'sono.' They are to be sung on the beat. I would practice this passage first slowly without them. When you are certain of the notes, add the acciaccature and gradually work the phrase up to tempo:

Io   so - no____   do - ci - le,

"Your sound for 'dolce, amorosa' should be warm. You must make the public think in the beginning that this girl is what she says she is. Do not split the second triplet as written between 'dolce' and the 'a' of 'amorosa.' Rather sing 'amo-' on the third triplet:

dol - ce____   a - mo - ro -   - sa,

"Again, on 'amorosa,' and later on 'mi fo guidar,' do not lose the tempo. Keep it moving right through the scales.

"There is also a tradition of carrying the low B of 'guidar' up an octave and anticipating the 'ma' which follows. Be certain you do not leave the low B until you have in mind the exact sound you want for the upper B, which should be like a smile, or like laughter from within. Do not make the portamento too slow, and there must be only the slightest hint of the *r* of 'guidar':

"On 'toccano' and 'debole' the pitch of the B and C-sharp must be clear:

"Be careful not to rush the downward scales on 'vipera.' This passage must have some bite to it. I would also add a bit of tension to the phrase by approaching the low G-sharp from the F-double-sharp below:

"For a lighter voice, the G to G-sharp will probably be too low, and an upper alternative would be more comfortable:

"The music can also be nicely varied when 'e cento trappole' is sung for the third time:

"Also, the scale downward on 'giocar,' just afterwards, can be opened up to raise to A:

(fa) - rò fa - - - rò gio - - - car

"Sing a full G-sharp at the cadence and build the note into the next cadenza. This is mine:

mi fo gui - dar._____ (ah)_____ ma, ma se mi

"As we have already heard the music for 'Ma se mi toccano' and 'e cento trappole' once, both phrases must be varied when repeated following the cadenza. But do not sing the same thing twice. Find a different variation for each. I think it is more effective if the first is simpler than the second. I sang this first:

toc - ca - - - no dov'- è il mio de - bo - - - le

sa - rò u - na vi - pe - ra,____ sa - rò____

And followed it with this:

e cen-to trap - po - le pri-ma di ce - de - re

fa - rò gio - car (ah)_____ fa - rò__ gio - car!

"With the second 'e cento trappole' you are back to the score as written. Watch the sixteenth notes on 'farò giocar.' Don't lose the rhythm or your tone here; these notes must be vibrant like a violin. Again, it is effective to end the phrase with an appoggiatura to the G-sharp:

"One last cadenza may be placed in the next measure on 'prima di cedere.' I used this one, which you can find in Ricci; if you use it, be sure the low C-sharp is open and not too covered:

"From here to the end, sing the music as written, except finish the aria by moving scale-wise up to top B. If you want time to prepare for the B, you can omit the last three turns on 'farò giocar' just before; if you do this, begin the final phrase on the F-sharp and sing it on 'ah':

"Some singers add a cadenza at the end as well, but there is no need for one. You have given the public nice high notes and good vocalizing already. Don't spoil these by adding something unnecessary. This will only take away from the expression and the sense of the piece. A simple ending is purer and cleaner; we enjoy your voice and we hear Rossini better.

ROSSINI ✆ LA CENERENTOLA

ACT II: *"Nacqui all'affanno"*

"Here we have a girl—Cinderella—who has suddenly come into her own after much abuse. Her sisters, who have treated her unjustly, are trembling, afraid she will now be unkind to them. Instead, she offers kindness, saying, 'In me, you will find a sister and a friend.' There is nothing tragic or heavy about this aria; her suffering is all behind her.

"In other words, this finale should be sung with tenderness and with beauty. It is not just a vocalise. When Cenerentola says, 'There will be no more unhappiness, no more anxiety,' it should be with affection and warmth—not overly brilliant, always ladylike.

"Rossini has marked the first phrase 'a piacere,' and it should be open, free and easy but with a nice shape to it:

Be careful not to slow down too much on 'soffrì tacendo.' Keep it moving:

The first cadenza must also have a good pulsation. Head directly to the A, but do not stay there too long or you will lose the overall motion of the phrase:

Here, and in the upcoming phrase, the fioriture must be very legato, very even:

ma per so - a - ve in - - can - - - to

Again, at 'come un baleno,' don't lose time. Give a good accent to 'come' to launch the phrase, then head straight for the top. I want the B given its full due, but no fermata. Move through it; your phrase does not end until 'rapido':

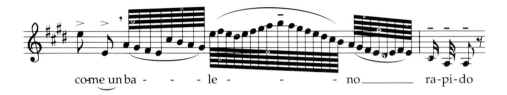

co-me un ba - - le - - - no_____ ra-pi-do

"There will also be a tendency to lag on 'la sorte mia.' Don't! Sing right through the phrase:

la_____ sor - te mi - a can - giò,

"End the second flourish on 'come un baleno' not as written but as you ended the first; it makes it stronger, more decisive.

"With the next cadenza, again head straight to the A. I would sing this, incidentally, on 'ah':

ra - pi - do   ah_____

"At the conclusion of the cadenza, go straight into 'la sorte mia'; do not let the phrase slow down. The music could well begin to drag at this point if you let it:

la sor - te mi - a, la_____ sor - te mi - a can - (giò)

"Next comes a change in attitude. Cinderella has told us her story, and now she reassures her sisters. Make the beginning very simple—no accents at first:

ACT II:
"Nacqui all'affanno"

No, no, no, no: ter - ge - te il ci - glio:

"Later, watch the accent on the last 'tremar.' Then, phrase down from the E and make 'perchè' very espressivo:

(tre) - mar, per - chè tre - mar, Ah per - chè?

"The vocalise at 'a questo sen' must also be sung without exaggeration, and I would sing it on 'ah':

sen, ah_____ te,

"The next phrase must be full; here she tells her sisters she will be a true sister:

fi - glia, so - rel - la,

When you reach 'tutto, tutto, tutto, tutto,' you cannot sing these four words in the same way. I would make a gradual diminuendo, accenting well the last 'TUT-to.' Watch the double *t*'s; let's have both:

tut - to, tut - to, tut - to, tut - to

End this section with a big and reassuring sound on 'trovate in me' to bring us into the finale:

ACT II:
"Nacqui all'affanno"

tro - va - te in me.

"There is a cut of twenty-three bars after the G of 'me,' from the bottom of page 342 of the Ricordi score—and always use Ricordi, if you can—to the bottom of page 345. It works like this:

"Make the little breaks in 'Non più mesta' without taking breaths. However, you will need a breath after 'fuoco' for the next phrase. And in that phrase —'starò sola a gorgheggiar'—sing firm trills, right on the note:

Non più mes - ta ac - can - to al   fuo - co

sta - rò so - la a gor - gheg - giar,   no.

"More than ever you will need a breath after 'fuoco' when the phrase is repeated in more elaborate style. The acciaccature here must be worked out very slowly and carefully so that they will be well articulated in performance:

fuo - co___ sa - rò so - la a_ gor - gheg - giar, no.

"Before the real vocalizing starts, make a slight ritard on 'fuoco' (the top of page 348); breathe well and think what you must do next, where you are going. Once you have begun the phrase, keep it light, and remember the accents on the offbeats; they will help give your singing shape:

fuo - co, non più me - sta ac - - - can - to al___ fuo - co___ sa - rò___

"When you reach the downward scales on 'Ah! fu un lampo,' go quickly to the A and attack it solidly; do not scoop to it! There must be no aspirates as you descend. Let the notes glide. Sing them within your breath and as much with your brain as with your voice:

Ah fu un lam - - - po,

"You must prepare technical problems, such as these scales and the acciaccature earlier, by working daily with the exercises of Concone and Panofka. These are a singer's bible. I would not use the Vaccai exercises; they are with words and are more advanced. It is the basics you must master first. If you practice Concone and Panofka, there will be no surprises for you in any music, and there must be no surprises if you are going to do your job as a singer properly. You must have your trills, your scales, your acciaccature. Believe me, if you were an instrumentalist and couldn't do technical things well, you would never pass an examination in the conservatory. It should be no different with a singer. There is no excuse not to have a trill, not to have even scales. We are, after all, just another instrument of the orchestra.

"To be a proficient vocal instrumentalist, you need Concone and Panofka. They are your homework as long as you are a singer. These studies will place your voice, will exercise it, will answer any questions about trills, gruppetti, acciaccature. They are not just for display—it is impossible to become a valid singer without them. It would be like a pianist attempting to perform without having worked on Czerny.

"Don't wait for someone to tell you to get these exercises. When I was young, there were many things I did on my own without being told to do them by my teacher. I brought new things to her already prepared. As a student, you cannot behave like a German soldier awaiting orders. Believe me, it will show in your voice whether or not you have practiced these exercises. Of course, they will be difficult at first, but later how easy things will be for you when you get to your scores! This is true not only of the bel canto but for all music—Beethoven, Puccini, Giordano.

"If you like, you may make slight variants in the fioriture, but only slight and within good taste. After all, what Rossini has written is hard work enough. Also, never embellish the first statement of a musical idea. Wait for the repeat.

"There is one final cut in this aria, one of a dozen measures from the top of page 351 to the bottom of page 353:

"At the very end, you may alter the line to rise to top B. This is, after all, the conclusion of the opera, and it can take a big vocal gesture:

ROSSINI ✦ GUGLIELMO TELL

ACT II: *"Selva opaca"*

"This is a love song, but do not take it too slowly or you will make your life impossible. Set a mood of agitation, of ardor in the recitative: 'I am alone at last, I hope to see him again; I hope that my heart has not deceived me.' Be certain to pronounce both *l*'s well in 's'allontanano' without breaking your line. Consonants will always be present, but you must learn to sing through them; they should never disturb the note:

S'al - lon - ta - na - no al - fi - ne!

Io spe - rai ri - ve - der - lo,

"Emphasize well 'Io TRE-mo, OHI-mè'—

Io tre - mo, ohi - mè!

—and sing the next phrase beginning 'Onde l'arcano' in one breath, omitting the rest written:

On - de l'ar - ca - no sen - ti - men - to es - tre - mo

di cui nu - tro l'ar - dor, ch'a - mo fors' - an - co?

"Wait until the orchestra has died away before speaking Arnoldo's name, then fill the phrase with feeling. Nearly always, one can take advantage of a name to emphasize and shape a line. Here, accent it—'Ar-NOL-do'—and then make a diminuendo. Also stress 'ch'io' in 'tu CH'IO bramo':

"When you reach 'Oh, almen ch'io possa confessarlo,' do not linger on the F of 'Oh.' Sing this phrase quickly, pointing it to 'Io T'A-mo, SÌ, t'amo, Arnoldo.' This is the moment that must be the most important, where you should make an effect:

"Each of the three phrases that follow ('Tu i giorni miei salvasti / e l'amor più possente / in me destasti') must be, in turn, one more expressive than the other. Even though you will breathe between each of these, you must keep the thought going as if there were no pauses. In this way, you will give the impression of one big phrase full of tension. You can even make a point of breathing, so that the public feels it; this will show the passion of Matilde's love.

"The aria must always be legato, not portamento. You must work out the pitches, particularly of the gruppetti, very slowly so that they are exact. Sing them as evenly as possible; no breath should escape in a gruppetto:

"There should be very little ritard before you begin 'alla calma'; do not let the music drag. The high A-flat of 'calma' must not be too weighted. The sound must reflect the word; it must be calm:

al - la cal-ma, al - la cal-ma, il mio cor s'a - pri - rà.

"The two matched phrases on 'l'eco sol,' I would begin piano and then make a crescendo on the E-flat of 'sol.' Be careful, however, on the second of these two to begin with a well-pronounced 'l'eco,' or it will not be heard after the forte just before:

L'e - co sol, l'e - co sol

"After these two phrases, I would inject some urgency into the next, not only because of the words ('my grief') but because this long phrase should end after the high A-flat, which is sung on 'ah.' This little trick serves both your needs and that of the music:

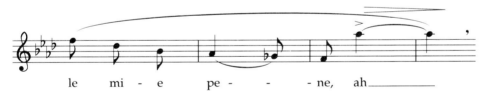

le mi - e pe - - - ne, ah

"The vocalizing which follows must be like oil, as legato as possible. Watch your rhythm on the turns; it would be easy to sing all sixteenths here instead of the sixteenth and thirty-second triplets written. Also, I prefer ending this phrase simply 'udirà,' instead of 'le mie pene udirà' as written, because there are too many words and the line is less smooth:

le - mi-e pe - ne u - di - rà, u - di - rà.

"In the second verse it would be nicer to sing 'Il mio passo vagando sen va' all in one breath. I know I am repeating myself, but I cannot stress this too often: when you have a long or difficult phrase, plan your breathing carefully and take time to draw in sufficient air:

il   mio____   pas - so___   va - gan - te___   sen   va,____

"Sing right through the notes of the coda; do not let the music become too strung out here:

(udi) - rà   es - so   sol   le   mie   pe - ne   u - di - rà,   u - di - rà,

"I would shape the final cadenza like this:

ah_____   sì   es - so   sol   u - drà.

Watch especially the two-note phrases before you breathe; they will give the line a last, lovely lift."

BELLINI ⨎ IL PIRATA

ACT II: *"Col sorriso d'innocenza"*

"Imogene in *Pirata* is very much like Norma; she is a terrified woman who has suffered a great deal, has known love and has had that love torn away from her. When a woman is less affected, the line of her music is sung less intensely. But intense or not, the line—and by 'line' I mean the arch of the music—must be smooth. There must be height to the tone; never let it drop. It is like an emotion which continually flows.

"One thing you must always remember in this music, and it is one of the first things Maestro Serafin taught me about bel canto, is that no matter what the note, how dramatic or light, you must always sing within the middle of it. There can be no slurring. There must also be a solid sense of a beginning and an end. In between, your singing must create the illusion of one large breath when in actuality it will be made up of many little breaths. If you are capable of doing this, you will take the public into another world, another atmosphere, a different spirit and mind.

"This 'mad scene' must begin very mysteriously. Imogene is delirious, weeping, out of her mind. It opens with a long, complicated recitative, and though it *is* recitative, you must respect the value of the notes or you will be unable to control the music.

"On 'potessi,' and throughout the aria where an appoggiatura is written, sing the appoggiatura and eliminate the note on which it leans:

"The next section is almost hushed, as if she is too frightened to speak:

"Emphasize well 'sepolta' when she asks, 'Am I in my house or in the *tomb?*'

"The next part is pure terror. It must be both on your face and in your voice. Watch well the interchange of whole and half steps in 'Geme l'aura d'intorno.' Make a careful distinction between them:

"Pick up the tempo at 'Ecco, ecco.' This must move quickly; she is hallucinating and thinks she sees her husband, Ernesto:

"A few bars later—'Ma, non è questo'—be very decisive and rhythmic. Also, wait for the fortissimo in the orchestra to die away before beginning, or you will not be heard:

Attack 'È desso' strongly and give a good emphasis to 'Ernesto':

" 'Ei parla' is much quieter; make it tender and piano. But even though it is piano, support your tone:

"Again, the tempo must move when you reach 'il figlio è salvo!' Plan it carefully; there is no orchestra with you, but we must always feel the beat:

And go quickly down the sixteenth notes of 'colpi':

"After 'vegga,' take a good, deep breath. Here the line broadens and becomes very espressivo. Watch the A-flat of 'mi.' An A-natural is an easy mistake to make here. I had trouble with this passage, and it is heavily marked in my score. You'll find you are never through studying your scores; there is always something to be learned.

"On stage, there will be many mistakes. Remember: a stage can make you, but it can also break you if you are not careful, because there you tend to go for big effects, to overdo, to push. So it is essential when you go home to look immediately at the music and try to gather together your thoughts about a performance. I remember I once found Maestro Serafin studying *Aida* the night before he was to conduct it. 'Well,' I thought, 'Serafin should know *Aida* by now,' so I asked him why he was looking at the music. 'You never know a score well enough,' he replied. 'There are things here that I did not see yesterday, and today I find them.' This is what music is all about; it is an everlasting search, not for power or glory but for what is deep within the notes.

"At the end of this phrase, sing with deep feeling 'anzi ch'ei mora'—'Let his father embrace the boy before he dies.' Don't linger on the B-flat of 'mora.' This is a difficult note for a soprano, or at least it was for me, because it lies in the passaggio. Get off of it before it thins out:

l'ab - brac - ci e mi — per - do - ni   an - zi ch'ei   mo - ra.

"Make sure you sing both *n*'s in 'innocente,' and don't lose your breath on the C. In the little cadenza that concludes the recitative I would eliminate 'tu'; the word is useless here. And sing 'per' on the thirty-second notes. I also would take the upper C at the cadence, then drop an octave to the lower C. Be certain of your pitch when you drop. If you are wrong, everyone will know it when the orchestra comes in with its fortissimo C:

Deh! tu, in - no - cen - te,   per me_____

_____ per_____ me   l'im - plo - ra.

"The aria, andante sostenuto, is very calm, but not too soft; it needs body. Attack the C well. In fact, before you open your mouth you must know exactly where the phrase is going and how long it will be. Keep it rhythmic; don't hold on to notes:

Col sor - ri - so_____ d'in - no - cen - za,

"In the triplets of 'perdono e di clemenza' be exact in your pitch and rhythm, or the phrase will smear. Breathe after 'perdono' if you need help here:

di per - do - no e di_____ cle - men - za,

"Sing the A of 'genitor' right on the note, emphasize 'deh,' breathe and sing 'deh fa-' on the triplet. It gives the line a nicer shape:

al ge - ni - tor_____ deh!_ deh_ fa - vel - la

"The vocalise on 'genitor' is difficult because of the repeated notes. If you do not phrase them well, they will not sound:

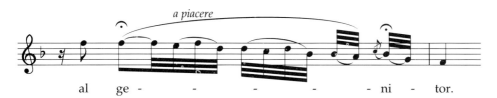

al ge - - - - ni - tor.

"In the next bars you have a demanding vocalise on 'Digli, ah! digli.' This passage must be worked out very slowly and rhythmically so that in performance it will move quickly and in tempo. There is no shortcut here, only hard work:

Di - gli, ah!_ di - - - gli_____che_ re - spi - - - ri.

"The problem of repeated notes returns in 'sei libero per me,' but it is more complex the second time. Work your phrasing out carefully. Believe me, it is difficult to put all these notes together and not sound like a machine, but that is our job:

ACT II:
*"Col sorriso
d'innocenza"*

di - gli che sei li - - - be - ro————————³ per me,—

"Get a good breath before 'a chi tanto' up to high A. I would sing the last F on 'ah':

a chi tan -   -   - to— ah— o - prò———

"There is a place for a cadenza at the end of the aria. The one given in the score has already been heard, and in the exact same form; furthermore, I think the aria needs more lift at the end than this short passage can give. I sing this:

(o) - prò,——   ah————————————

————————— sì per - te— o - prò

"In the next section, you must be very generous with your voice—really open it up:

Qual suo - no fe - ra - le

"Take the upper A on 'eccheggia,' and watch 'rimbomba.' Most scores have a misprint here; the C and the A should both be quarter notes:

ec - cheg - gia,   rim - bom - ba?

"After the chorus has sung, be careful with the phrase 'Spezzate i suoi nodi.' Be very exact here; don't let your emotion pull this phrase out of shape. Always guide phrases where you want them to go:

Spez - za - te i suoi no - di, ch'ei fug - ga

" 'Il palco funesto'—the funereal scaffold—needs special coloring. This will not be easy the first time, when it is sung on D:

Il pal - co fu - ne - sto

But the second time, it is sung lower, on G, and 'funesto' especially should have a dark color:

Il pal - co fu - ne - sto

"Just before the cabaletta begins, breathe well after the 'ah!'; then ride the B of 'sì' up to C, take a quick breath, and you're off. Make the cabaletta full but rhythmic:

ah!   sì_____ Oh, So - le! ti ve - la

"The chromatic scales at 'd'angoscia,' which I would sing on 'morrò,' must be precise, but like a cry from the heart:

ACT II:
*"Col sorriso
d'innocenza"*

mor - rò_____   d'af - fan - - - no,

These scales are not light and pretty. They must be filled with drama. Look
at your score—Bellini has instructed they be sung 'con gran forza':

d'af - fan - - - no,_ d'or - ro - re

"In place of the scale up to C that ends this series, I would sing instead
this:

(d'or)- ror   Ah!   mor - rò

Also, at 'Là, vedete,' I would go up to D and then C, rather than the A to
G written. Also, alter 'il palco funesto' to a downward arpeggio. All of this
heightens the tension of the scene:

Là,   ve - de - te   Il   pal - co   fu - ne - sto

"This is one cabaletta where it is good to repeat the second verse because
it is more bound into the music than is usually the case. But the second time
must be varied for interest, though not so much that we lose the sense of
Imogene's terror. Here are my variants:

ah!   sì___ Oh, so - - le! ti ve - - la

"These must be sung with great thrust and animation. The high C could be easier on 'morrò' instead of 'Ah! sì.' It depends on your voice. Use whichever will give you a good note.

BELLINI ❧ LA SONNAMBULA

ACT I: *"Tutto è gioia"*

"Though this aria is brief—its repeat is usually cut in performance—it is not just a lovely bit of singing. There is bitterness here. Lisa sings, 'All is happy, all is festive, and I must be happy too, even though I am miserable.' She is losing, you see, the one she loves to another. So there is a sharp, even furious quality here. In the score you will see that Bellini has marked many accents, and instructs that the final phrases be sung 'di forza'—with force. So, you must let your voice out, you must sing with passion.

"In the first phrase give good color to 'gioia' and to 'festa':

"When you reach the A-flat, take time to breathe, so that your throat will be open; sing right on the note, with a good attack:

"The next phrase—'O beltade a me'—must be strong; she is speaking of the beauty that has lured her Elvino away:

Come down quickly off the B-flat that follows and head the phrase directly to the fermata. The E-flat, D, and D-flat here must be given importance and must push into the return of the first theme:

"Respect Bellini's 'di forza' at the end with a breath after 'deggio' and a good attack on 'accarezzar!' Put a fermata on the second D-flat of 'accarezzar' for a final emphasis:

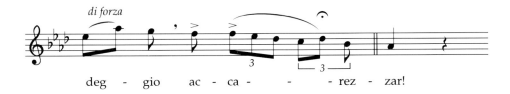

ACT I: *"Come per me sereno"*

"This aria is sung by Amina, a young girl on her wedding day who is bursting with happiness. She greets her friends and looks about her, saying, 'How could a day be so beautiful?' But remember, this is a simple, a shy girl; hers is a quiet joy. There must be radiance to your singing, but it must also be sustained and unaffected.

"Don't spend too much voice and breath in the recitative. Give it life, keep it moving, but let it be easy, like conversation. Always the vowels must come out; be very conscious of the words. For example, caress well 'teneri amici' [tender friends], and be careful not to make the usual elision with 'che alla gioia' but sing two separate words here, 'che/alla':

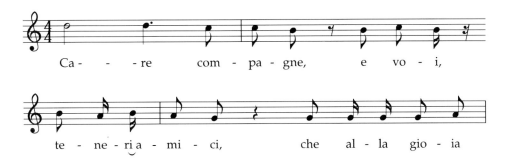

"In some scores you will see a fermata on the F of 'il vostro amore,' but the emphasis and the fermata should be on the G. This is part of the Bellini style:

che v'in - spi - ra   il_____   vo - stro a - mo - re!

"Later, in 'dolce pianto di gioia,' you can use a nice, expressive portamento from the D of 'pianto' to the A of 'di' and then stress well 'GIO-ia':

dol - ce   pian - to   di   gio - ia,

When you come to the second 'pianto,' make the turn fast, and then again accent 'gioia':

pian - - - to   di   gio - ia,

I like the upper F in 'e quest'amplesso,' because it separates the first recitative from the change of mood (andante con anima) that follows:

e   que - sto am - ples - so

"Once more, remember to make 'teneri amici,' when it returns, very espressivo; Bellini has written here 'con tenero accento'—with tender inflection, or tender accent. You must give it to him:

Com - pa - gne   te - ne - ri a - mi - ci

"The beginning of the aria must be very sustained yet with a feeling of almost floating. Watch well the B-natural of 'sereno'; make the pitch clean:

Be careful to pronounce both *r*'s in 'terren' and sing a clear triplet on 'come fiorì.' Triplets are extremely important in this type of music and lend a special character to the vocal line; never slight them:

One other small but important point: we must hear all three vowels in the middle of 'bello e ameno.' Put a fermata on the B-flat of this phrase and think of the note as divided in two on which to sing 'e' and the 'a-' of 'ameno':

"The next phrase—'Mai, mai di più lieto aspetto'—must also be very espressivo:

Begin the phrase up to high C on 'ah' and place the 'non brillò' on the D-flat and on the scale that follows:

Be certain this embellishment is rhythmically exact but still flowing. Often when one sees many little notes one gets terrified. But there is no reason for this if you divide them carefully within the beat and within the phrase. Practice such passages slowly until they are comfortable. The same is true of the trill on 'non brillò' which follows. This is a difficult trill because it is on a whole tone. We must hear both the E-flat and the F equally well vibrated:

non   bril - lò;

"The A-flat of 'amor' which follows must be approached directly and cleanly, and give good emphasis to 'mio' at the end of the phrase:

co - lo - rò, a - - - mor del_____ mio,_

"Do not linger on the B-flat before the cadenza but rather stress the A-flat that follows it:

(colo) - rò,_____ a - - - mor

"The cadenza is a matter of your choice. You will find a number given by Ricci which various singers have used. I do not particularly care for these, because I feel they are not within the mood of the aria. Once, singers were very free with cadenzas; they used them for vocal fireworks. But if you care enough for the composer, and you are willing to take the time, you can create a cadenza that is within his style. The one I used recalls the aria, because it is built on a phrase that occurs early in the piece:

(a) - mor,   ah_____ 6 _____   ah_____ 6 _____   sì

ah_____ sì   del   mia a - mor

"If you make your own, be certain to write it down so that you will have it exactly. These things should be set in your voice and your mind and not left to chance."

BELLINI ✍ *NORMA*

ACT I: *"Casta diva"*

"In this scene, according to my thinking and that of Serafin, Norma is dominating the savage, ferocious people she serves as priestess. They are crying for battle with the occupying Romans, but Norma wishes to avoid war at all costs. She has broken her vows as priestess, taken a Roman lover, Pollione, and borne him two children. So she must somehow avoid open conflict yet keep her people appeased. This she does through the ritual of 'Casta diva.'

"In the recitative, when she says, 'I see into the future; the Romans will not be destroyed by us but by themselves,' I don't think she is all that sincere; she is only stalling. This is a woman frantic for time, and you can imagine how strong she must be in order to dominate her people and quiet their cries. As 'Casta diva' is a consequence of this domination, the aria's lines must be kept very peaceful, very silvery, as a contrast to the powerful recitative just before.

"This is one of the most difficult of all arias, not only because a fine legato is essential but because you are so vocally exposed. Also, the aria comes early in the opera, while you are still nervous and not yet fully into the performance.

"Though 'Casta diva' is of a single, sustained mood, there are many small details that make up this mood and must be correct. For example, in the very first measure—

Andante sostenuto assai

Ca -   -   - sta___

—there must be a good, clean attack on the A of 'Casta.' This is one of the basics of bel canto—attacking a note straight on. The attack must always be solid and well supported, even if you are singing pianissimo.

"In this first measure, we also find a characteristic feature of Bellini's writing which must be highlighted. Nearly always, Bellini prefers scalewise ornaments to chromatic ones. Look at the turn on 'Casta,' written out in the first measures and also occurring in the third measure, though not written out there. It moves down by a whole step, not a half; in other words, it goes to G, not G-sharp. When Bellini wanted a half tone instead, he was always careful to write it in. With Rossini and Donizetti you can usually assume a half step in an ornament, but never with Bellini. It is important that the pitch here be very clear so that this special feature of his writing can be heard.

"This opening page of 'Casta diva' must be kept very smooth, very clean, with all the pitches exact and covered with a good legato. Be particularly careful not to change the color of your voice while singing the ornaments; they should be a single sound. Incidentally, watch the repeated C's on '-genti'; we must hear both:

"At the bottom of the first page, before you start up the scale to that string of high A's, take time for a good breath and sing the scale on 'ah':

When you reach the A's, make a good attack on each, and take a deep breath before the last to carry you over to the B-flat. Remember always to take advantage of such a breath for the sake of expression. In this instance, it not only gives you a good B-flat, but it helps make the ritard needed to end the phrase and provide a crown for the line. Coming down from the B-flat, the final phrases must be stretched a bit, again for expression. Place a slight fermata on 'senza' just before the chorus's entry:

"Norma's embellishments over the chorus should be sung on 'ah,' and once again exact pitches are essential, as is a good legato. This is especially true when you have chromatic scales:

ah

These must be performed as an instrumentalist would—clean and clear.

"For the second verse of the aria, begin with less tone but make certain it is well supported; again, a good attack on 'Tempra,' right in the center of the note. The balance of this verse goes along much like the first until you reach the cadenza at the end. Sing the chromatic scale on 'ah,' and take the traditional upward ending to F; it gives more shine to your voice and to the line:

tu fai,   nel   ciel

Some conductors, however, may wish you to sing the ending like this:

tu fai,   ah   nel ciel

While I prefer the first, I understand the second and have sung it as well. There is, after all, a chorus singing with you, and this second ending helps the conductor hold the ensemble together. By your making a clear break before 'nel ciel,' the chorus knows when to move with you.

"The first real change in mood we have in this scene comes with the cabaletta, 'Ah! bello a me ritorna.' Its recitatives are big, like those before 'Casta diva,' and should be as well weighted. In particular, hold on to the F of 'Cadrà' so that it pushes you into 'punirlo io posso':

Allegro

Ca - drà   pu - nir - lo io   pos - so

Here, Norma is reassuring her people that Pollione, the Roman proconsul, 'will fall. I can punish him.' But she adds quickly under her breath, 'Ma punirlo il cor non sa' [But the heart does not know how]. These phrases must be highlighted, because they are our first awareness that Norma is living a double life, which will eventually bring about her downfall.

"Keep the cabaletta light and use a good, even legato. On page 75 of the Ricordi score there are two instances in which you may vary the vocal line. I prefer the alternates; and on the second and fourth beats of the first, I sang quarter notes rather than a second gruppetto of sixteenths:

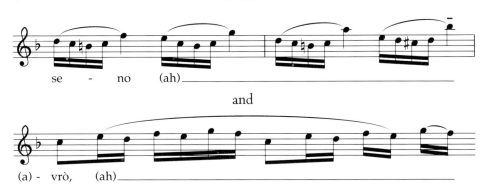

"After the scale down from C, there is a traditional cut—and this, I think, is good tradition—of four pages (Ricordi, pages 76–79), which eliminates the second verse. Why good? Because rarely is a melody such as this interesting a second time, and we must not risk boring the public.

"When Norma enters after the chorus ('Ah! riedi ancora'), put an accent on 'QUAN-do'—*when* I gave you my heart':

The tempo must also slow down a bit here for emphasis, but return to tempo with the sixteenth notes that follow.

"If you like, there is a place for a nice high C to conclude the aria. Instead of the written B-flat, the C can be approached from the lower A like this:

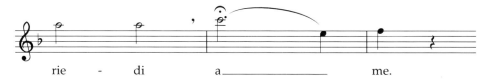

I like the C because it is an heroic gesture by Norma and brings the scene to a strong conclusion.

ACT I: *"Sgombra è la sacra selva"*

"This is a small aria—actually, a recitativo and prayer. There are no enormous vocal gestures here, yet there must be a pull of terror underneath the outer calm. Adalgisa is terrified of being a priestess in love with a Roman soldier. The recitativo contains her many thoughts, her guilt and her love.

"Observe each of the indicated appoggiature:

Sgom-bra è la sa - cra sel - va, com - piu - to il ri - to.

"In a long recitative such as this, there must be certain parts that are highlighted to give the whole shape. One of these is 'quel fatal Romano'— that fatal Roman. Move this along:

quel fa - tal Ro - ma - no,

Also give more on 'Irresistibil forza'—irresistible force:

Ir - re - si - sti - bil for - za qui mi tra - sci - na

And fill 'e di quel caro aspetto' with warmth, because she does love him:

e di quel ca - ro a - spet - to

"Make the prayer itself very sustained, and in the second phrase don't stay too long on the fermata. Once you have the note well, come down quickly:

Deh! pro - teg - gi-mi, o Di - o!   deh!___ pro - teg-gi - mi,_

"We must emphasize 'perduta' each time it appears. 'I am lost,' she sings. 'God have pity on me.' Be sure to breathe after 'perduta':

per - du - ta, per - du - ta___ io son,

On the last one, the G-flat, I would sing 'ah' and phrase down, moving the 'per-' to the A:

Ah_____ per - du - ta io

ACT I: *"Va, crudele"*

"The scene between Adalgisa and Pollione which follows her prayer is rather straightforward. What is needed here is that the music be kept alive rhythmically. Do not let the tempo down at the end of phrases; this can easily happen if you are not careful to move ahead.

"Pollione is a warrior throughout, always confident. He knows he has Adalgisa even when she has her doubts. He must begin the scene quickly and with authority; he is giving an order to Flavio, dismissing him:

(Ec - co - la!   va,   mi la - scia,   ra - gion no o-do)

"Adalgisa must be kept on the light side; never pound out her notes. We need a good firm sound, however, at 'Io l'obbliai'—she has forgotten their love:

"Pollione must sing deep within the words and give us a good G, which can be held, at the end of the first section:

"Be careful not to rush the sixteenths on 'mai rinunzia' and afterwards. Use them to show his determination:

"Later (Ricordi, page 101), when Adalgisa sings the same notes, they must be light and free:

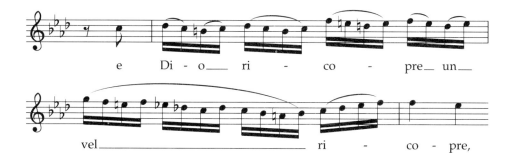

And the A-flat that follows should be easy, not pushed. When you come off it, do not linger on the next A-flat, but put your fermata on the D-flat instead:

ri - co-pre un vel,　　or per me___ ri - co　-　pre___ un vel.

"Before the second duet, Pollione should sing the 'Adalgisa' each time with great expression—he wants her to run away with him to Rome:

A - dal - gi - sa!　　A - dal - gi　-　sa!

"Page 106 is cut entirely, and we go from Adalgisa's 'o l'error perdona almen' straight into page 107, like this:

(l'er) - ror,___ o l'er-ror per-do-na al - men.　　A - dal - gi - sa!

"There is one more cut on the last page of the duet—only two measures, but it tightens up the ending. Leave out the measures with the quarter notes, and at the very end, Adalgisa can take the upper A-flat. Pollione may join her if he wishes:

a te sa - rò, a te, a te sa - rò,

sfi - dar sa - prò, sfi - dar, sfi - dar sa - prò

BELLINI ⌘ I PURITANI

ACT I: *"Ah! per sempre"*

"This aria for baritone demonstrates that the bel canto composers expected and got as much *abellimenti* from men as they did from women. However, few male voices now have this sort of flexibility. People excuse this by saying, 'Well, he's a dramatic baritone.' It seems today we classify singers according to what they can or *cannot* do. Consequently, we have the basso cantabile, basso profondo, soprano leggiero, lirico leggiero, lirico spinto, lirico I-don't-know-what.

"Once upon a time, however, one soprano sang *Norma, Puritani, Sonnambula, Lucia.* She was a soprano—*basta!* I have a poster in my home of an evening with Maria Malibran in which she sang both *Sonnambula* and *Fidelio*! It's a matter of technique. Today, if a soprano does not have her high notes, she is a mezzo. But we all must have our high notes, our low notes. We must have everything.

"Can you imagine a violinist without his high notes, his low notes, his *abellimenti*? 'Cantabile'—what does this mean? It means you have a singing tone. But we all must be cantabile, not just basso cantabile but baritono cantabile, soprano cantabile. We must also sing what is written. How do you get out of notes which are there, staring you in the face? You must have your trill, your acciaccature, your legato; otherwise don't call yourself a singer.

"In the recitative to the aria, be careful to pronounce well; let's have all the words with good vowels.

"At the end of the andante affettuoso, do not observe both the fermate. Rarely in Italian opera are two fermate performed together; usually, the first is omitted. You may add an F to heighten the line if you like:

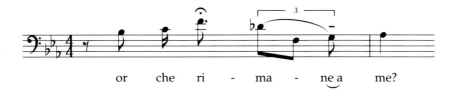

"Though the aria is marked larghetto sostenuto, you must give the tempo a quick feeling so that it will keep flowing. Sing out; bring authority to this music:

"As a low voice such as a baritone tends to be heavy in texture, there will be a temptation to slow up for the embellishments. But you must sing right through them or the aria can fall apart; phrase 'm'avanza' like this:

"Give a bit of emphasis to 'piena di dolor,' when Riccardo says, 'My life will be filled with sadness':

"Watch 'ventura'; both times it is embellished. These are two more spots where the aria could begin to drag:

"Phrase 'affanni nella speme' as you did 'm'avanza sarà piena':

"When 'affanni nella speme' is repeated, take a quick breath before 'nella,' but within the tempo:

(af) - fan - (ah) - ni__ nel - - la__

"I think the cadenza is a bit long and can be simplified somewhat. But whatever you sing here, head straight through to the last note. Plan it carefully.

ACT I: *"A te, o cara"*

"This aria is a love song. It must be ardent but with pureness of sound. It must also have a rolling rhythm to it so that it always flows.

"Begin piano, but with an open throat. Singing softly does not mean that you close in on the tone. When you reach the second 'amor talora,' I would eliminate the rest after 'talora' and take a breath after 'guidò.' This way you can carry the phrase through the sixteenth notes on 'pianto' with greater ease. Be careful, though, not to slow 'pianto' down; make it nice and legato but within the tempo:

a - mor ta - lo - ra mi gui - dò fur - ti - vo e in pian - - - to,

"Emphasize well 'tra la gioja' on the F-sharps, and, again, keep your line moving, in this case straight up to the A. Don't wait too long on the A in the first verse; it can have more stress the second time around. This time push on to the C-sharp of 'esultar' and hold this note instead:

(d'ac)- can - to   tra   la   gio - ja, tra   la   gio - ja e   l'e - sul -

- tar,   tra   la   gio -   ja e   l'e -   sul - (tar)

"If you sing this aria in concert, at this point you will go directly to the second verse. This is very demanding; at least in the opera the verses are separated, and there is some opportunity to rest yourself in this difficult piece. The second verse contains a top C-sharp, and you must prepare carefully your approach to this note and your exit from it. I would suggest this:

l'o - ra,   se ram-men-to, se ram-men-to il mio tor - men - - - to,

"Also, in the last bar of the aria before the chorus returns, you can change the line to ascend to a B. It is more beautiful this way. But don't overdo this phrase. Sometimes singers make an elaborate turn on 'palpitar' as well as after the B. There are certain liberties that can be taken with this music, but this is not one of them. Keep the line clean:

(palpi) - tar   m'è   più   ca   -   ro   il   pal - pi - tar.

ACT II: *"Qui la voce"*

"Opera is filled with people who go mad, but, interestingly enough, they go mad in different ways. This will affect how their music is performed. For example, Elvira in *Puritani* loses her mind for only a short while. The man she is to marry runs away with another woman on their wedding day. Actually, he is rescuing the imprisoned Queen of England, to whom he owes allegiance, but Elvira does not know this at the time. When he tells her the truth, her sanity is restored. So her madness is temporary, whereas Lucia is ill from the start. Her first aria, 'Regnava nel silenzio,' must have a sick quality about it; it must reflect the dark moors of Scotland and her mental frailty.

"You must consider all of these things when you prepare a role; you must try to characterize the person you will play, decide what sort of individual she is, what her background is, what her attitudes must be. This you will get from the music, not from history. History has its Anne Boleyn, for instance, and she is quite different from the Anna Bolena of Donizetti. So you cannot go by history; you must make your decisions about her from the music. In the same way, it is Lucia's music that tells us she is doomed from the start. Elvira, on the other hand, is a healthy girl; her madness can be, and eventually *is,* cured by love. Bringing any of these roles to life is not simply a matter of singing notes well. That is for school; there you are primarily concerned with notes. But after school, you must be concerned with giving notes expression, of bringing meaning to phrases.

"This mad scene is very sustained and dependent on a good command of rubato, that give-and-take which is the lifeblood of romantic music. Don't try to scale this music down. Let your voice out, be generous, give notes full importance. And be careful of the pitches; they must be well defined within your legato. Usually with musicians, one ear more than the other controls pitch. With me, it is my right ear. Find out which it is for you, and learn to use it to hear your faults and correct them, to control your quality, your color.

"The first part of the scene is marked largo, but it must flow. Remember, tempo is a question of attitude, and your attitude is what is most important. You can give a slow tempo a gay attitude, just as you can be tragic within a fast tempo. You might find a conductor who will have strong ideas about a tempo and take the music faster than is comfortable for you. But you can save yourself and the situation by striking a slower attitude within his fast tempo. You do this through the way in which you handle your sound, the way you weight the words.

"Remember, the introduction to 'Qui la voce' is sung offstage, so it must be full in order to carry. Also, it is 'ren-DE-te-mi,' not 'ren-de-TE-mi,' and sing a good portamento on 'speme.' You must love such phrases with your voice, love them dearly. You may have difficulty singing clean vowels on 'speme'; I would think of the *e*'s as being mixed with *ah.* It will bring you closer to the *a* sound you want:

"At the end of this phrase and throughout the aria you will find a falling interval on 'morir.' This must always be very expressive. Take your time, do not rush the B-flat to G and later the B-flat to E-flat:

"Sing the acciaccatura on the second 'O rendetemi' slowly as well. Use it to emphasize the sadness of this scene; her unhappiness must be not only in your voice but on your face as well:

"On the first top A-flat, do not change color on 'speme'; never aspirate on the A-flat here. I would also carry the A-flat down to the lower C-flat before beginning 'O lasciate-.' Take a good breath after 'lasciate-'—let out the old air and put in fresh, so that you will be prepared for the long phrase coming up.

"Incidentally, in this matter of breathing, I feel strongly that no one should breathe high in the chest. I am not a voice teacher, but I know this can choke you. You must breathe lower, entirely from your diaphragm. This is easily said and not easily done, of course, but it is the very basis of singing well. Good diction also places your voice where it should be. The clearer your diction, the purer your sound, the better the public will hear you and the better your interpretation.

"Be careful coming off the A-flat of 'lasciatemi.' Don't rush this little cadenza; it must be *appoggiata* with legato. Remember, too, to phrase well 'morir':

"The aria itself, like the introduction, must be sustained. Do not start it too softly. Remember: it has a beginning, an arch, and an ending. One section flows into the other to form a whole. No one note must stick out too much; hold to the line. Everything must have its proper proportion. There cannot be a sudden forte or piano to take us outside of the line. This will destroy what you have built.

"The aria is passionate; it must vibrate in order to have expression and meaning. I would not use portamento on the E-flat octave from 'voce' to 'sua,' though in general this aria needs portamenti or it is dead. Watch carefully the many vowels of 'sua soave.' We must have them all but without a change of position in the voice. One must melt into the other. Also accent well 'mi chia-MA-va,' and head the line to the F:

Qui la vo - ce sua so - a - ve   mi chia - ma - va

Don't be afraid of singing full, firm low notes here and elsewhere. You must, if this aria is to come alive.

"One phrase especially in need of rubati is 'e poi crudele ei mi fuggi.' Sing this exactly as a fine pianist would play Chopin. Make the acciaccatura and gruppetto of 'crudele' very expressive and precise in pitch. Also, move the fermata of 'fuggi' from B-flat (as in the score) to A-flat. Measure carefully your rubato. It must be free but yet have a pulsation to it:

poi cru - de - le ei mi_____ fug - - gi

"At 'Ah! mai più' [Ah! nevermore] put her despair in your voice:

Ah!   mai   più

"On the repeat of 'qui assorti insieme,' you can omit the final *e* of 'insieme' when you portamento to the G, if this is more comfortable in your voice. Also, give the public all the joy of 'gioia'—'GIO-ia,' it should be. This will help you as well by strengthening the line of your singing:

qui as - sor - ti in - siem'_____   nel - la   gio - ia

"On the last 'speme,' do not pull back; let your voice out. You must dominate this phrase:

spe - me,_____ o la - scia - te, la - scia - te-mi mo - rir.__

"When you sing this aria in concert, it will be necessary to cut from the final 'lasciatemi morir' (Ricordi, page 174) directly to the cabaletta (page 182, one bar before the allegro moderato).

" 'Vien, diletto' is in the same mood as 'Qui la voce'; Elvira's mind is still clouded. In general, I think cabalettas should not be sung too lightly, and this one should have maximum legato.

"You will notice that there are very few staccati here. Bellini is very careful to write in staccati when he wants them; don't add them if they are not there. His is a very legato style of music. Even when Bellini writes staccato, it is more *appoggiato* or sostenuto than, say, Donizetti.

"Be careful not to lose the two low E-flats that begin the cabaletta. They must be full:

Vien di - let - to è in ciel la lu - na

Give good emphasis to 'la LU–na,' and make certain not to separate the notes of 'tace' and 'intorno.' Always, always think legato. Put the arch of the music in your brain:

tut - to ta - ce in - tor - no, in - tor - no

"The scales must also have no separations. Let the words go by; sing on 'ah':

gior - no, ah_____ vien,_ ti

ACT II:
"Qui la voce"

"When you come to the first cadence, bring as deep a feeling to 'mio cor' as you brought to 'morir' in the cavatina. Save your fermata for the end of the phrase:

po - sa, vien ti po - sa sul mio cor!

"Be free with 'Arturo mio' and even freer with 'tua Elvira.' Ignore the alternative notes at 'essa piange,' and breathe well before beginning this phrase:

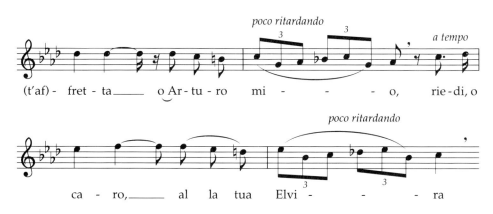

(t'af) - fret - ta____ o Ar - tu - ro mi - - - o, rie - di, o

ca - ro,____ al la tua Elvi - - - ra

"Again, sing the descending scales on 'ah.' In the chromatic one, do not linger on B-flat but come swiftly down—clean pitches, no separation—and point the line back to the F:

ah____ a - mor.

"Next, there is a cut that removes the second verse of the cabaletta and takes you to the middle of page 187:

(a) - mor, al - - - l'a - mor____

"The chromatic scales on the next page must be worked out slowly. They should glide effortlessly—no accents. Cut 'riedi' after the last chromatics before you begin the final scale upward:

"You may end the scene on an E-flat if you like and then cut the next eight bars like this:

But remember that singing is more than high notes, however nice they are. What good is a high E-flat if everything before it has not been beautiful and well sung? The note should come as a natural consequence of all before it."

DONIZETTI ✌ *LUCIA DI LAMMERMOOR*

ACT I: *"Regnava nel silenzio"*

"There has been a trend recently to overornament music of the bel canto school, and particularly that of Lucia. This I condemn, because the less you ornament this music the closer you will come to realizing its drama. This is especially true in 'Regnava nel silenzio.' You must make the public feel that this girl is ill from the beginning, so this aria is the key to the drama that follows. It shows the unsettled mind that later leads Lucia to murder her husband.

"She recounts to Alisa, her companion, a terrible dream she has had in which the water of a fountain turned to blood. This is frightening, and you cannot tell someone of such a nightmare with ornaments you would use for Dinorah's Shadow Song. There are, of course, certain changes you can make in the music, and certain notes you can add that are of a good tradition and which will heighten the drama.

"I have heard people say that tradition is last night's bad performance. But tradition does exist, ways of performing music that are passed on from one generation to another. Tradition is good or bad depending on who has had good taste and who has not; good taste is that which respects the spirit of the composer and his music.

"Musically, this aria is a twin to the first-act aria for Leonora in *Il trovatore,* 'Tacea la notte placida.' It reminds us once again that the same singer who sang Lucia and Norma also sang Leonora, and that for Lucia you must have the same concentration of sound and the good low notes you have for Leonora.

"Returning to the question of tradition, there are a number of small changes in the recitative to this aria which are good and which add to the mood of the music—appoggiature on 'sappia' and 'periglio' and later on 'veggo' and 'sai':

Ed-gar-do sap-pio   qual ne cir-con-da   or-ri-bi-le pe-ri-glio

and

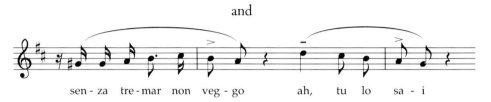

sen-za tre-mar non veg-go   ah,   tu lo sa-i

"Because this is recitative, there is a certain freedom open to you, and I would emphasize the G-sharp after 'quella fonte' when Lucia first speaks of the fountain in her dream. This is terror; it must be in your voice:

Quel-la fon-te   ah_____   ma-i

"Keep 'Un Ravenswood, ardendo di geloso furor' rhythmic, and point the line to the F-natural of 'fisse.' 'E l'infelice cadde nell'onda' must also be strict, so that it has shape, and add another appoggiatura when you reach 'sepolta':

ed   i - vi   ri - ma-nea   se - pol - ta:

"Also, you may raise the E of 'ascolta' an octave, resolving it back down to the lower E:

A - scol - ta.

"The cavatina must be not too slow and as legato as you can make it. Remember, a note is round; it has a center. No matter what passion or emotion you are dealing with, whether the note is piano, as here, or forte, you must sing purely, in the middle of the note. The only exceptions are when a composer asks for a portamento or a glissando. Do not confuse legato with slurring. Slurring, or sliding, will ruin the rhythm, affect your diaphragm and breathing after a while, and your technique will suffer. I know it takes an effort to remember to keep the line clean, but believe me, it will be less effort in the long run. The first five phrases of this aria are legati within bigger legati:

"If you can manage it, it would be better to sing 'fra l'aure udir si fè, ed ecco' all in one breath. If this is too difficult, breathe after 'udir,' because 'ed ecco' needs to be well accented:

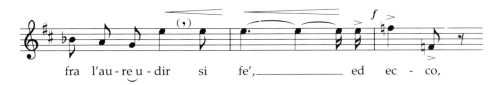

"Take a deep breath and sing 'ecco su quel margine' quickly. I would alter the end of the scale for better emphasis, as below, and sing it on 'ah.' Sing 'ah' also on the upper G. Do not linger on the low F ('me') but go at once to the upper F and make it short. This is also an expression of Lucia's terror, of the horror of her dream. And it must be 'mo-STRAR-si':

"Be careful at 'e con la mano' not to rush the A. Sing it in tempo and lean on it somewhat before descending:

"'Stette un momento immobile' must be very rhythmic and build steadily to 'dileguò.' Make a diminuendo on the scale, pause a moment on the B-flat, and breathe before beginning 'e l'onda pria':

"Watch your pitches carefully on 'limpida'—and make it like the word, limpid—and again on 'di sangue rosseggiò':

"You must have good trills on 'ah pria sì limpida'; these show Lucia's fear:

Learn your trills slowly. We must hear two notes in equal vibration. When practicing, attack the written note, then vibrate little by little both notes, gradually increasing the speed. If you study in this manner, you will be able to attack a trill evenly, right on.

"The cadenza at the end of the aria is *a piacere,* but it must be *a piacere* with good taste. Remember that your cadenza should reflect the words that

Lucia has just sung—'The waters so limpid turned crimson as blood'—so there is no room for anything cute or for a display of fireworks. Mine was built mainly on scales:

ah———————————— sì, di san-gue ros-seg - giò

"After Alisa has finished, Lucia begins an entirely new mood. She is no longer in her dream; she now thinks of her happiness with her lover, Edgardo. This is one of the few healthy glimpses we have of this unbalanced woman. So attack 'Egli è luce' well, and sing the remainder of the recitative quickly. Again you may alter 'è conforto' to include a top B; it will set the change of mood. Also, I would make a small ritard on 'penar':

(con) - for-to, ah— è con-for-to al— mi - o, al mi - o pe - nar.

"The cabaletta is like a theme with variations. As both verses are sung, the second must be altered, for the public has already heard this music once. As a rule, happy music can take more variants than unhappy music. When you state the theme, do not peck at the notes; once again, sing very legato:

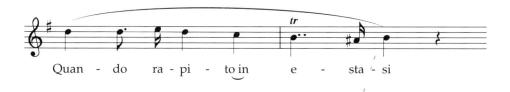

Quan - do ra - pi - to in e - sta - si

"Accent well 'giura' when you come to 'mi GIU-ra eterna fè' [he *promised* me eternal faith]. Make the second 'eterna fè' very elegant; it should float:

mi giu - ra e - ter - na fè, e - ter - na— fè,

"Another word that must be highlighted is 'gioja.' It is always important whenever it appears. Sustain well the D of 'pianto' which follows. This D lies awkwardly in the voice, or at least it did in mine, and it may give you trouble. If you feel you need extra breath, breathe just before 'il'; it would be better, however, to manage the phrase in a single breath if possible:

"Watch the chromatics on 'd'accanto'; they must be clean:

"In the vocalizing that follows ('il ciel per me'), some singers prefer to sing both B's and both A's, though the notes are tied. But whether you separate them or not, the entire phrase must not be broken up; take only one breath before. Be certain you don't lose time coming off of the B and the A; keep the music moving:

The same is true when the phrase is repeated. I would alter the scale on 'schiuda' to end on the lower G. It is easier and more rounded. Also, eliminate 'il ciel' in the middle of the scale; it is not necessary. Sing the scale on 'ah':

"Take time to make the re-entry of Lucia on D very expressive—a nice messa di voce, for example:

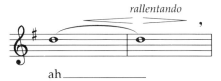

"With the return of the cabaletta you begin the variations. Keep them simple at first, although later they can be a bit more extended; any repetition should be more elaborate the second time. Sing your variants on the words, and, again, do not slow down the music to accommodate them. I used these for the first two phrases:

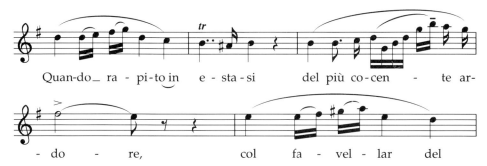

" 'Mi giura eterna fè; gli affanni miei dimentico' is sung as written; you do not need to vary every note. I used these variants next, though it would be perfectly permissible to sing 'parmi che a lui d'accanto si schiuda il ciel' as written:

"As I said, repetitions must contrast, so when you reach the second 'il ciel per me' it should be heightened—like the variant I used, for example:

"Again, sing the downward arpeggio on the last 'per me' down to G. Then there comes a cut of twenty bars to take you to the coda, like this:

"Lucia re-enters on G, sung on 'ah,' and a D in alt may be added to bring the cabaletta to a brilliant end:

ACT II: *"Il pallor funesto"*

"This duet might seem lightweight to you at first, but it isn't. In fact, the baritone must have the same power, the same attitude as in *Un ballo in maschera*. Just because *Lucia* is Donizetti and not Verdi, don't lessen your power. From the beginning, there must be great strength to Enrico's music. He has done everything possible to force his sister, Lucia, into a marriage with a man she doesn't love. Now he confronts her with enormous authority, ready to crush any resistance. In other words, he is on the lookout for trouble, he is aggressive.

    "Sing fully from the start with good accents: 'Ap-PRES-sa-ti, LU-ci-a':

    "I would eliminate the quarter rest in 'Sperai più lieta' and sing both phrases as one:

    "Accent well 'FA-ci' and 's'ac-cen-do-NO':

    "Also, I would add a portamento on 'taci' for further emphasis:

    "Lucia knows that her brother is the enemy of Edgardo, her true love, so she must begin her part of the duet defiantly. Keep the rhythm very steady here, and sing on the words with good accents: 'Il pal-LOR fu-NES-to or-REN-do':

Later, stress well 'il mio strazio, il mio dolore.' This must be as dramatic as you can make it—'See my torment, see my pain':

On 'rigor,' I would make a portamento down to the B before beginning 'perdonarti.' This will strengthen the phrase:

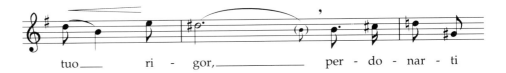

When you reach the F-sharp, I would not sing it on 'ah' as written but rather sing the phrase on 'l'inumano.' There is also a cut here of six bars. Jump forward to the dotted rhythms:

"As this duet is so tense and so unhappy a section of the opera, make as simple a cadenza as possible. This is no place for a display. Also, breathe well before 'dolor' to accent Lucia's anguish:

"Enrico is like a snake here. Though he tells Lucia 'You are right, I was cruel to you' and seems to be forgiving, he is still thinking of himself, still determined to compel Lucia to marry Arturo. So, even as he is saying 'I am your loving brother,' there must be a hardness to the line, very rhythmic. Accent well 'indegno' and 'affetto':

quel che t'ar - se in - de - gno af - fet - - - - to;

As in Lucia's part just before, there is also a cut of six bars for Enrico to the dotted rhythms:

l'in - sa - no a - mor, l'in - sa - no a-(mor)

The short cadenzalike passage at the cadence should be well emphasized. Enrico calls Lucia's love for Edgardo insane, and the cadenza is a summing up of this:

tu l'in - sa - - - no a - mor.

"When he begins to speak of Arturo—'Nobil sposo'—Lucia interrupts him; and 'Cessa, cessa' must be nearly frantic:

Ces - sa, ces - sa!

"Enrico answers her with increasing anger, and 'Basti' is almost shouted; it is like an order—'Enough!':

Ba - sti!

"After she reads the forged letter Enrico has prepared, which makes Edgardo appear unfaithful, Lucia's G must be desperate. Hold it, and wait after releasing this note before singing 'il core mi balzò' [my heart jumps]; make this phrase very espressivo:

"I would sing Lucia's phrase 'la folgore piombò' in one breath, omitting the two written rests; it will be more poignant:

"The larghetto, 'Soffriva nel pianto,' must be sung like a great violinist would play this passage, in other words, with intense and deep feeling:

"It is important to highlight 'la VI-ta' and sing 'riposi in un cor' with urgency, pressing the phrase forward. Then, breathe and return to the tempo on 'l'istante di morte,' accenting well 'l'i-STAN-te di MOR-te':

On the long notes sung on 'me!' do not diminish too soon, and make certain of the change of pitch from E-natural to E-flat. I would also add a portamento down to F before beginning 'quel cor infelice':

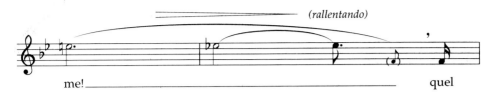

me!_____ quel

"Enrico begins 'Un folle t'accese' very secco, almost cruel. He knows he has crushed Lucia:

Un   fol - le   t'ac - ce - se,   un

"In the duet the pitches must be carefully worked out between the soprano and baritone. Both must listen to the other and carefully tune their notes:

Lucia:

L'i-stan - te__ tre - men - do è giun - to__ per__ me,____ sì,

Enrico:

Un fol - le__ t'ac - ce - se, un per - fi - do a - mo - re;

"The words should be changed where both reach the fermata, so that a fresh attack can be made following the hold:

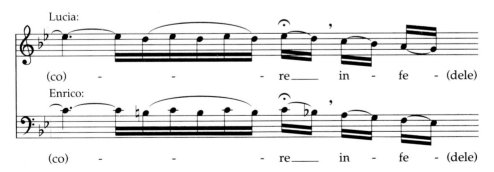

Lucia:

(co) - - - re__ in - fe - (dele)

Enrico:

(co) - - - re____ in - fe - (dele)

"The cadenza also requires careful planning, like this:

ACT II:
pallor funesto"

"The next section, vivace, must move without letup until the meno allegro. Enrico should accent well 'M'odi! Spento è Guglielmo.' He is afraid Lucia will continue to defy him and he will be ruined without Arturo's wealth. This comes to a head with 'Salvarmi devi!' [You must save me!]. Lean on these words forcefully:

"Again, strongly accent 'Devi salvarmi,' and when Lucia sings 'Ma—' cut her off ferociously. After Enrico's 'il devi,' Lucia must wait until the previous sounds have disappeared. Sing 'Oh ciel! oh ciel!' with great emotion but clean, well-supported tones:

"Enrico must begin the vivace with a well-weighted sound, legato, but forceful and with good accents:

To reinforce this stance, I would portamento from the last note of the meno mosso back into the first tempo:

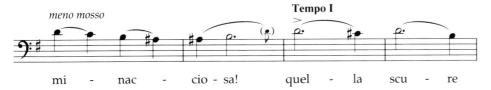

"While Lucia maintains the tempo at her entry, 'Tu che vedi il pianto mio' should be sung with a sad, slow attitude; phrasing is very important in achieving this. Place your tone well within the words:

"A big cut follows, fifty-two bars, but without it the momentum of this last section is lost. There are some conductors today who would like to open up everything, open up our hearts if they could. But this is too much on a singer. We are not machines, and there are usually good reasons for cuts—mainly, they help retain the audience's attention and strengthen the drama. This cut works like this:

"When singing together, watch the triplets. They must be well articulated and rhythmically as one:

ACT II:
"Il pallor funesto"

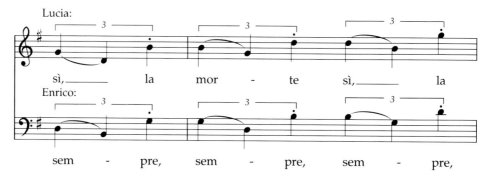

"I would again slightly change Enrico's words on the last 'sempre.' Move 'in-' from C to B so that both can take a breath at the same time:

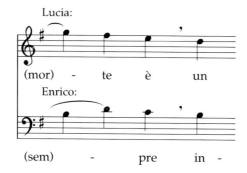

"Another cut follows, this time of twenty bars, and we jump to the last thirteen measures of the cadence, like this:

"I would only sing two of the three phrases on 'è'un ben' and 'a te,' because you will need a measure or so to rest before the very end. Here high notes can be added, a D for Lucia and an F-sharp to G for Enrico. This is the climax of the piece, so why not? Later on, when you are old and no longer have these notes, you'll hate yourself for not having used them! But also remember, they are not to be used without a reason.

"High notes such as these must be measured; if you hold them too long, the public will tire of them and you will have spoiled your effect. Be certain that both singers leave their notes together. Being a bad colleague means holding on to a note longer than the other singer. Being a good colleague means finishing at the exact same moment:

ACT II:
"Il pallor funesto"

DONIZETTI ⤷ *ANNA BOLENA*

ACT II: *"Al dolce guidami"*

"Once again we have a 'mad scene,' and like that in *Pirata,* there are many changes of attitude, many disconnected thoughts, many different atmospheres. One moment she is saying 'Why are you crying?' The next is brighter—'Oh!

my wedding day.' Then she is frightened, then sad, and so forth. It is always *cambiare, cambiare*—changing—and it takes many colors to bring these moods alive. Also like the *Pirata* scene, there are a lot of recitatives before the aria. It must not be sung too slowly or you will not be able to sustain the music. With the exception of certain moments that are more important than others and must be highlighted, keep to the rhythm; the music will come easier, you will have more breath, and the effect you make will be lovelier.

"Be sure to accent 'voi' in the first phrase: 'Piangete VO-I?':

Pian - ge - te vo - i?

"There are several places here where appoggiature are needed and not written—on 'nozze,' 'tosto,' 'l'impose':

noz - ze.   to - sto   l'im - po - se.

"In the scale down from high C, do not hold the top note too long. I would also exchange the words 'infiorato l'altare'; sing instead 'l'altare in-fiorato' and omit 'è acceso':

l'al - tar - e   in fio - ra - (ah) - - to

"Later, it is 'il crin m'or-NA-te.' This and 'del mio serto di rose' must be a single phrase, so do not waste time on the G, and do not let the repeated notes of 'mio serto' drag you down:

il crin m'or - na - te del mio ser - to___ di ro - se.

"Several marked changes of attitude come quickly: 'Che Percy non lo sappia,' then 'Oh! chi si duole,' and finally a very agitato allegro. The orchestra will be moving swiftly and will gradually make a crescendo. Lean on the appoggiature here, with good accents, so that the words carry above the orchestra:

Do not sing 'sgrida'; drop the *s*:

"Sing through the rests on the high G on 'ah.' Tie this note to the second G. If you repeat it, it will cut the power of the first G. I would also phrase down to F on 'ah,' then sing 'mi perdona':

"Try to make 'infelice son io' as espressivo as possible—'I am unhappy' —even with a tear in the voice:

"At the end of the next phrase, 'Toglimi a questa miseria estrema,' take the time to make 'estrema' important, not only because of the sentiment ('extreme misery'), but to clear the air for the next change of mood, which comes immediately:

mi - se - ria   e - stre - ma.

"In the allegretto, give good emphasis to 'fia'—'Don't *let* me die here deserted':

non   fi - a, non   fi - a che qui de - ser - ta

"Sing the notes as written for the cadenza 'oh gioja':

oh   gio - - - ja!

This is a very dramatic scene, and you must not fool around with its mood. There will be time for fireworks later.

"The aria is very legato. Be careful not to let little technical things, such as the triplets, drag down the music. It must always flow. These ornaments must be within the line and on the word:

Al   dol - ce   gui - - -da - - - mi

"As this is a highly ornamented aria, one way to prepare for its difficulties, such as 'ai verdi platani,' is to breathe well before a new phrase and use this breath as a source of expression. Offer the breath to the public as drama; in actuality, you are preparing yourself to sing the next phrase evenly and with a good sound. Such little tricks make it possible for artists to present themselves and the music in the best light:

"When you reach the quasi–cadenza on 'ancor,' do not linger over individual notes but point the line down to the C. When you go up again (C-sharp, D, E), you can give more emphasis. I would also ride the E into the F of the next phrase before pronouncing the 'Ah!':

"Notice that when the words 'Al dolce guidami' return, the musical phrase on which they are sung is repeated a bar later, down a third. There should be contrast between these two parallel phrases. I would make the first forte and the second piano. I would also remove the rest after 'guidami' and add an appoggiatura on 'natio':

"It would be better to sing the acciaccature on 'amor' as thirty-second notes, making the rising chain of notes all thirty-seconds. Otherwise, the line will become too choppy. The sentiment here, after all, is love:

"Be very expressive with 'un sol.' I would take it slightly out of tempo, then return to tempo for 'nostro amor.' Then, take time again for 'un giorno':

"Sing the notes written for the little cadenza; there is a bigger one coming up where you will have more freedom. Also, sing it on 'Ah! un giorno':

"As was the case with 'Come per me sereno' from *La sonnambula,* I built my cadenza for *Bolena* here out of a previous motif:

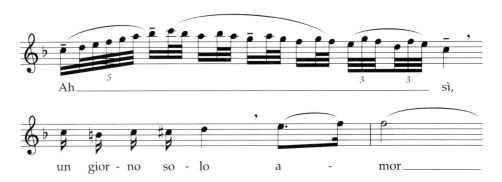

Do as you like; just be certain it is not too much, and in the right spirit.

"Incidentally, omit the C on 'del' just before the cadenza. It is really not needed."

DONIZETTI ✷ DON PASQUALE

ACT I: *"Quel guardo il cavaliere"*

"This is a lovely aria, but I have heard many people overdo it, try to make it cute, with all sorts of exaggerated portamenti and coy pronunciation of words. No! There is enough spirit in the music, especially with the acciaccature in the allegretto, to bring it to life. There is no need to add more. Sing the opening with a good legato, the second half with lightness and taste, and everything will be fine.

"Incidentally, there is something I have wanted to mention for some time: I have often heard a singer clear her throat before beginning an aria such as this. Please don't do this; it only scratches your vocal cords. Often you will have catarrh, but it will leave as you sing. Clearing your throat will not get rid of it; it only acts like a grater on the cords.

"As you begin this aria, remember that Norina is reading to herself, so your singing should be somewhat subdued, piano. The first spot to watch is the D to G of 'cavaliere.' No portamento here, just a good legato:

There is a great difference in connecting notes by a legato and by a slide. We use the latter, but sparingly and only for drama's sake. Otherwise, it can become a bad habit.

"As in the *Anna Bolena* aria, there will be a temptation to slow the music down for gruppetti. Be careful not to do this. For example, in 'son vostro cavalier' you must give some emphasis on the C-natural; Donizetti has made it a dotted note, but if you stay on it too long, you will lose the flow of the line:

The little cadenza on 'paradiso' begins slowly and gradually increases in speed:

(para) -di - - - - - so

'Giurò che ad altra mai' should be big. Begin at least mezzo-forte, crescendo, then diminuendo on the F-sharp of 'mai' and crescendo again on the E:

giu - rò   che   ad   al - tra   ma - i

As you will have broadened the phrase here, return to tempo with 'non volgerìa,' but pause on 'il':

non___ vol - ge - rìa   il   pen - sier.

"The two laughs are difficult, but you can make them easier by singing the notes as written. We must hear exact pitches; sing them lightly:

Ah, ah!   ah, ah!

"Be very careful that the many acciaccature of the allegretto are clear; they are what give this section its humor:

So an - ch'io   la   vir - tù   ma - gi - ca

This entire allegretto moves in and out of tempo all the time. These shifts must be well planned and none of them exaggerated or the aria will become too heavy:

bru - cia - no i co - ri a len - to fo - co; d'un

bre - ve sor - ri - set - to co - no - sco an - ch'io l'ef-

- fet - to, di men - zo - gne - ra la - gri - ma, d'un

su - bi - to___ lan - guor. Co - no - sco i mil - le

mo - di del - l'a - mo - ro - se fro - di, i

vez - zie l'ar - ti fa - ci - li per a - de - sca - re un

cor. D'un bre - ve sor - ri - set - to co - no - sco an - ch'io l'ef-

ACT I:
"Quel guardo il cavaliere"

-fet - to,   co - no - sco,   co - no - sco,   d'un su - bi - to lan -

- guor;   so an - ch'io la vir - tù   ma - gi - ca   per   in - spi - ra - re a -

- mor,___   co - no - sco l'ef - fet - to ah_____   ah___

sì   per in - spi - ra - re _ a - mor.

As you can see, it changes nearly every phrase.

"Be certain to make 'Conosco i mille modi' bigger than the rest, even serious, and the first 'per inspirare amor' should be very legato. Finally, do not lose time on the scales; they should be swift. Point the second directly to 'sì' and then head straight for the fermata.

"The words are very difficult in the next section, and you must work at making them clear without distorting the rhythm:

Ho te - sta biz - zar - ra, son pron - ta, vi - va - ce

You can take more time with 'Se monto in furore'; this should be big:

Se mon - to in fu - ro - re,   di   ra - do sto al se - gno,

Begin the trill—it is a whole-note trill—right squarely on the F. It must be as even as possible:

"When the acciaccature return, there is a cut of sixteen measures from the end of bar two in the second stave of page 36 (again, Ricordi) to the third bar of the fifth stave:

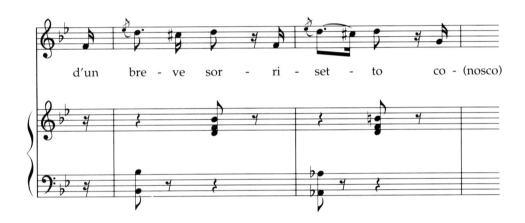

"After the scale down from B-flat, you may add a cadenza. As I do not perform this aria, I have no cadenza of my own, but something like this would be appropriate:

"Take time to breathe very well before the high B-flat at the end; then the aria cuts to the last seven bars of page 38:

(a)   - mor.

VERDI ✑ *NABUCCO*

ACT II: *"Tu sul labbro"*

"This aria must be sung with solemnity; it is a great priest offering up a prayer. Your sound should be round, firm, and always vibrant; the attitude is a monumental one.

"In the recitative, sing with sharp rhythm and accent 'LE-vi-ta':

Vie-ni, o Le - vi - ta!   Il san - to co - di - ce re - ca!

I would animate 'di novel portento'; let the power of your voice out:

Di no - vel   por - ten - to   me vuol mi - nis - (tro)

Here and in 'me servo manda,' don't chop up the syllables; keep the vowels flowing. Also, make certain on 'd'Israele' that the low C is as full as the upper C:

Me ser - vo man - da,   per glo - ria d'I - sra - e - le,

"Even though 'Tu sul labbro' is to be sung sotto voce, Verdi has accented the first notes. In other words, he wants this music sung firmly, with importance:

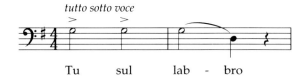

Vibrate the sound well, make it rich, on 'parla or tu col labbro mio,' and don't close up the *o* of 'mio':

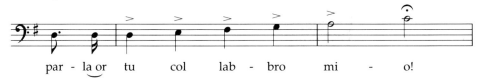

"Again, 'E di canti' must flow. Here and until the end of the piece the rhythm must be precise to convey Zaccaria's authority:

Move through the cadenza on 'sorgerà' without losing too much time:

What needs emphasis is the final phrase down to low G. This can be stretched. Also move the fermata from B to A:

VERDI ⤳ *ERNANI*

ACT I: *"Ernani, involami"*

"Elvira in *Ernani* is sometimes sung by light voices, but her music, especially this aria, is for a dramatic soprano, for a *Trovatore* or *Forza* voice. It is heavy work and needs power. It is dramatic music sung by an unhappy woman who is being forced into a marriage she does not wish. Here, she cries out for her true love, Ernani, to take her away. Your voice must be well weighted.

"As always in recitative, keep the line moving. Do not be tripped up by the gruppetti; sing through them:

Watch the interval on 'Ah! non'; it does not move scalewise but skips a third:

In 'che quale immondo spettro,' if you lean well on the two *m*'s and the two *t*'s, you will see how much more dramatic your phrase will become:

And let's have good, full low notes on 'ognor m'insegue.' This low writing is one thing that makes this aria so difficult for a light voice:

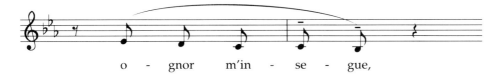

Let your voice out on 'col favellar d'amore' with authority, and don't forget the two *l*'s:

col fa - vel - lar d'a - mo - - - re,

A good sound is needed on 'Ernani'; open your throat and sing right through the sixteenth notes to the F of 'core':

più sem - pre Er - na - ni mi con - fig - ge _ in _ co - re.

"The aria cannot be sung lightly or with a smile in your voice. She is saying 'Ernani, take me away from this horrible place.' You must put this thought into your throat.

"Be precise with the turn; go to it immediately. Also, you must breathe after the first 'Ernani!' not only to emphasize his name, but to prepare for the turn so that the phrase will be well rounded. Here and throughout the aria, be certain you do not hold on to the last note of the phrase too much:

Er - na - ni!   Er - na - ni, in - vo - la - mi

"I would not sing the staccati on 'd'amor concesso'; they will make the line too choppy. Keep it always legato:

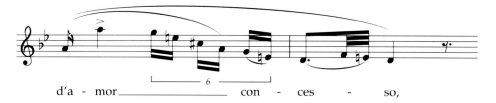

d'a - mor_____ con - ces - so,

The same is true of 'ti seguirà' which follows.

"Begin 'Un Eden di delizia' piano and build the phrase to the B-flat. Be careful with the two-note phrase coming down; phrase into the accent:

Un E - den di_ de - li - zi - a sa - ran_

"Sing through the vocalizing on 'saran quegli antri a me.' The line should always move towards the low B-flat. Do not give too much on the high C here; you will have a chance to show that you have this note in the cadenza:

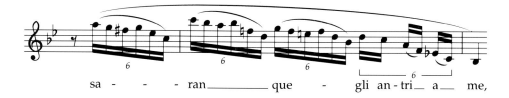

sa - - - ran_____ que - gli an - tri a_ me,

"Next, you have two phrases on 'un Eden.' Sing the first forte, and on the second a messa di voce. Then, portamento down to the lower F, piano:

un E - den, un E - - - den,

I have heard some sing a trill on this second phrase, but it is wrong. To me, Verdi is a god, and whoever distorts his music is not a serious artist. If you want a good example to follow in this music, listen to the recording by Rosa Ponselle.

"Sing the cadenza on 'ah.' You may hold the C, but then move swiftly through to the G-flat. Sing the finale on 'un Eden a me'; it will be cleaner:

Ah_____ un E - den a me

VERDI ✤ *LA BATTAGLIA DI LEGNANO*

ACT I: *"Quante volte"*

"This aria is strange Verdi, with strange intervals, so your pitch must be very exact. Give your voice generously from the beginning; the sentiments are patriotic.

"Keep the recitative moving. If you allow it to slow down, you will lose the tension. Accent well 'amo'—'I LOVE my country'—and again 'l'amo':

a - mo la Pa - tria, im - men - sa - men - te io l'a - mo!

"You must also underline 'sotterra giacciono'—'my brothers, my parents have been buried':

Sot - ter - ra giac - cio - no

After 'parenti,' speed up the next phrase ('e troppe in sen'):

e trop - pe in sen m'a - per - se or - ren - do fa - to

" 'A me soltanto' is calmer. At the cadenza, go quickly to the C-flat. You must be perfectly in tune from C-flat or the entire effect of the cadenza will be lost:

con - for - - - to, con-for-to il pian - (to)

"The major difficulty of the aria—and, believe me, I know, because I wanted to record this piece and still haven't—is to keep its detail and yet have the whole expressive and under a long line.

"Begin it serenely, with a good legato:

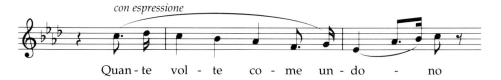

You will not have much time for the trill on 'la morte,' so attack it head on, and let the gruppetto take the full quarter beat:

"The words 'funesta' and 'tomba' both require strong feeling, and Verdi specifically asked for a portamento between the two. After this portamento, accent well 'TOM-ba':

"After 'volea,' come down from the E-flat of 'ah' slowly, hold the D-flat, then breathe deeply before starting 'Ah! per me':

I would also breathe again after 'rea,' because you have a long way to go in the next phrase. Sing the cadenza on 'ah'; give Verdi the 'lunga' he asks for on the B-flat, but leave the note quickly and push the phrase to the F of 'brama' before breathing again:

ACT I:
"Quante volte"

re - a —— ah —————————— fin la bra - ma

I would also breathe before 'fin la brama' up to A-flat and again before the 'la brama' that follows. I suppose you could sing the long passage down from A-flat in a single breath, but to me it then becomes just vocalizing, and these are very dramatic words: 'I would have wanted to die if I didn't have a child.' So I would breathe before it to give a more tragic expression:

re - a fin la bra - (ah) - - ma —— la ——

"Try to sing the final cadenza in one breath, on 'ah,' and take a generous breath before 'morir':

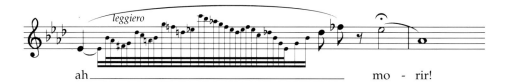

ah ———————————————————— mo - rir!

VERDI ❧ *RIGOLETTO*

ACT II: *"È il sol dell'anima"*

"This duet—or, rather, scene—should be begun by Gilda calmly, with not too alive a vibrato in her voice. However, when Giovanna asks Gilda if she dislikes the young man who has been following them to church, Gilda answers with a forte 'No.' Her next phrases—'no, chè troppo è bello, e spira amore'—must be generous in sound. I would begin each forte and then diminuendo:

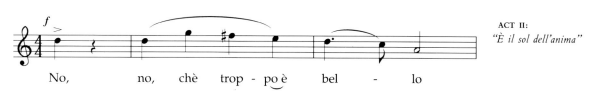

No,   no,   chè   trop - po è   bel   -   lo

"Do not make 'Signor nè principe' marcato; the rhythm should be precise, yes, but the phrase very legato. The sound must not be childish:

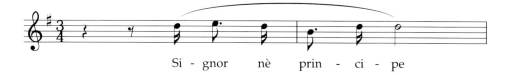

Si - gnor   nè   prin - ci - pe

"You will have difficulty accenting correctly 'sento che povero.' This phrase is badly written, I'm sorry to say. I do not understand why Verdi gave more stress to the second syllable of 'sento.' In speaking, it would be 'SEN-to,' and in singing you must accent it this way. However, the long note is on the second syllable, so you will have to work around this, perhaps by making this long note more piano:

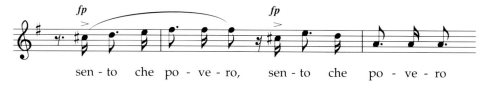

sen - to   che po - ve - ro,   sen - to   che   po - ve - ro

"I know I have said repeatedly to be sparing in your use of portamento, but there are a number of places in this scene where portamenti are necessary. After all, these are two young people very much in love. Their phrases must be warmed up, and a good way is to use portamenti. When Gilda says, 'Awake or asleep, I call to him,' I would *portare* the D to G of 'chiamo' [call]:

So - gnan - do o   vi - gi - le   sem - pre   lo   chia - mo,

"Next, Gilda must sing 'e l'alma in estasi gli dice' with great enthusiasm and fullness. Be sure to cut off the G of 't'a—' as soon as the Duke sings. His 'T'amo' must have extreme warmth, and I would make a generous portamento on the octave down from G:

ACT II:
"È il sol dell'anima"

"The allegro vivo should be sung impetuously, but do not overdo the top A. Sing it in tempo, with a short fermata on 'ciel':

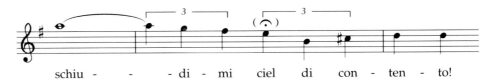

"The next phrase for Gilda is an interesting one. To me, she seems desperate, but not really. Neither is she coy. She says 'Is there no one here to help me?' while secretly happy that the young man she has been noticing in church is finally at her side. You can convey this idea by undersinging her music at this point and by making a portamento on 'nessuno' [no one]. This portamento will, in a way, contradict the idea of the word and get her state of mind across to the public:

"Later, when she says 'Uscitene' [Get out], it must also have a yes-and-no coloring:

"The Duke's next phrase must be very passionate, with a good accent on 'ac-CEN-de-ne':

O - ra che ac - cen - de - ne

Don't be too rhythmic with 'Ah, inseparabile d'amore il dio.' It is like a small recitative passage before the duet begins and must have great warmth. Sing 'DI-o' and 'FA-to':

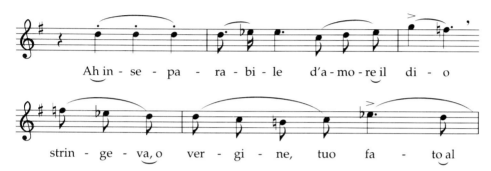

Ah in - se - pa - ra - bi - le   d'a - mo - re il   di - o

strin - ge - va, o   ver - gi - ne,   tuo   fa - to al

"The duet is filled with subtle, small shifts of tempo and mood. For example, you have to take time with each turn; they must be slow and expressive. To do this correctly will require rubati:

sua   vo - ce è il   pal - pi - to del   no - stro   co - re

I would also stretch the line at 'che agl'angeli più ne avvicina' so that the top A can be emphasized. Also, add an appoggiatura for '-cina,' breathe, then sing the F on 'ah':

che a - gl'an - ge - li,   a - gl'an - ge - li   più ne av - vi - ci - na   ah!___

"The next phrase ('Adunque amiamoci') is difficult for a tenor as it rises scalewise to a B-flat. Before you begin it, think high, point the line. Verdi also asks that it be sung stringendo, which means pushing the line forward. If you do this, it will make life easier and give the phrase more ardor, more urgency:

ACT II:
"È il sol dell'anima"

"Gilda enters the duet piano and with a very smooth sound. During her first phrases, the Duke must be careful to sing more piano than she does, and to allow her time for her turn on 'sogni.' In duets such as this, you must always correct your dynamics according to your colleague. If he or she has a less strong voice, then adjust your sound. Never overpower a colleague. If by nature a colleague's voice is big, you will need to make certain that your sound is clean and pointed, so that it will penetrate and not be lost:

"Later, when Gilda reaches 'Ah! de' miei sogni' it must be sung marcato and not too softly, for here the Duke's line must dominate but Gilda's counterpoint must not be lost. Her line is actually a legato-staccato. It must carry:

"The held notes at the end of the duet are marked pianissimo but they must still have warmth. Vibrate the sound:

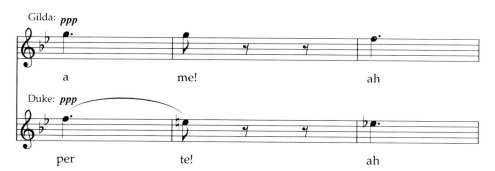

"The cadenza is always cut down. It is too long and out of character as it stands. Sing only its final phrases:

"After the cadenza, the Duke should accent well 'Che M'A-mi, DEH! ri-PE-ti-mi,' and Gilda should answer him with a forte and diminuendo to piano when she confesses her love. His next phrase, 'Oh me felice,' must then be an outburst of happiness:

" 'Il nome vostro ditemi' should be very serious, no coyness:

"When the Duke answers, it should be somewhat breathless. He has been caught off his guard when Gilda asks his name, and he has to make up an answer:

"The vivacissimo at the end must go like the wind and has to be carefully prepared with clean, clean diction. Give close attention to the dynamics or everything will run together, and be certain not to lose the acciaccature:

"There are several traditional cuts at the end of this duet, beginning after Gilda's scale up to B-flat. You should perform the ending as follows. Incidentally, Gilda usually sings a D-flat at the end. The Duke may join her as well if he has the note and is comfortable with it:

ACT II: *"Caro nome"*

"This aria must be sung with a pure sound; it must be like crystal. It is as if Gilda is in a dream, thinking of her Prince Charming.

"Begin softly, but be certain your tone is supported; a piano must be as well supported as a forte:

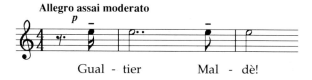

Give more voice to 'nome di lui sì amato' as she tells us that his name is the name she loves; crescendo on the F-sharp:

As you will need a breath after 'ti scolpisci nel core,' sing only 'cor'; 'cor' and 'core' are the same in Italian. I would also make a slight portamento from the B to A-sharp of 'innamorato' and then a diminuendo. If you cannot keep the sound of the last A pure, let it go:

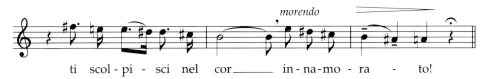

ti scol-pi - sci nel cor____ in-na-mo - ra - to!

"Before you begin the aria, fix well its attitude in your mind and on your face. Lean on 'Caro,' though do not make it strongly accented. The eighth rests between 'nome,' 'che il,' 'mio,' and 'cor' are not pauses for breathing; they are for emotion. They are typical of Verdi. Make them felt, but keep them within your phrase. The attitude here is the same as that in 'Ah! fors'è lui,' the first-act aria from *Traviata:*

Ca - ro no - me che il mio

"There are several places where portamenti should be added. After all, Gilda is a passionate girl—remember, she sacrifices her life for love at the end of the opera:

cor fe-sti pri-mo pal-pi - tar, le de-li-zie del-l'a-

- mor mi dêi sem - pre ram-men - tar!__ Col pen-sier

"Watch the accents on 'il mio' and 'desir'; attack these two-note phrases and then diminuendo:

(pen) - sier il mio de - sir____

"After this, you have two different kinds of trills, and a clear distinction must be made between them. The first, on 'sempre volerà,' are attacked on the principal note. The second, on 'l'ultimo sospir,' have acciaccature and begin above the principal note. In between the two, let your voice out on the F-sharp of 'volerà'; really vibrate here. I would ride the F-sharp up and put a fermata on the G-sharp. Also, after reaching G-sharp, change your 'ah' vowel to 'e':

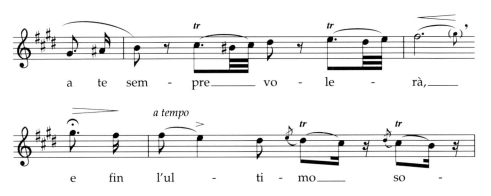

Another portamento is needed on 'sospir':

Come down quickly on the small cadenza of 'volerà,' then make a rallentando as you go up. Breathe well after the C-sharp, and attack the G-sharp on the button. The note can be nice and long:

The next phrase should almost float, and move 'sospir' to the triplet:

You can also hold the C-natural in the next phrase. End 'nome' on the E to D-sharp, then begin the A-sharp on 'ah,' adding 'caro nome tuo sarà' at the end of this phrase:

" 'Col pensier il mio desir' should have a nice lift to it, just as in the opening of 'Ernani, involami.' Keep the high A-sharp to B-natural within your phrase:

"Sing the cadenza from A on 'ah,' and do not stop on the low B but head the line back up to the A-natural:

"The vocalizing that follows should be on 'ah' as well; make it deliberate and be careful of the intervals. This passage should be practiced slowly and mechanically until it is set in your voice:

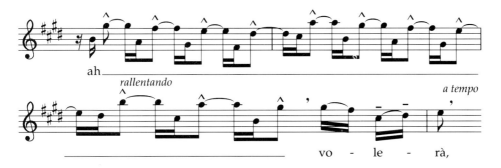

"On the next series of two-note phrases, which are all even, make a crescendo and diminuendo on each group and accent well 'sospir':

(vole) - rà fin l'ul- ti - mo so - spir,   fin l'ul- ti - mo so - spir,

The last set, rising to G-sharp, I would sing on 'ah':

ah_____ ca - ro__ no - me,_tuo sa - rà,__

"Also, sing the C-sharp scale on 'ah'; don't lose time here. Begin quickly, and keep the scale animated as you go up. Take a real breath before the low A-sharp, and sing 'caro' on this two-note group. Finally, accent well 'tuo':

(sa) - rà,___ ah____

_____ ca - ro no - me, tuo sa - rà,

"Be certain before the triplet on 'volerà' not to cheat us of the acciaccatura:

vo - le - rà,

"The cadenza should be on 'ah.' I sang this one, which is a bit different than the one in the score and more effective, I think:

tuo,___ ah_____

_____ sì, ca-ro no-me, tu - o sa - rà.

ACT III: *"Cortigiani, vil razza dannata"*

"You must be fiercely savage, like a blind animal when you sing this tragic aria. Rigoletto would like to kill the courtiers who have stolen his daughter but must instead beg them for her return. Thus, he hates himself as well for *having* to beg. Yes, there are moments of great legato here, but these must have an underlying tension that shows Rigoletto's burning emotions. Sing the notes, of course; but forget your voice as such. Think first of the drama.

"Rigoletto begins by calling the Duke's courtiers 'a vile, damned race.' He asks them what price they got for his daughter ('mio bene'). 'There is nothing you wouldn't do for gold,' he shouts at them, 'but my daughter is a priceless treasure.'

"Take the beginning very quickly—with a very choppy quality—but give it great impetuosity. Bite into the words: 'COR-TI-GIA-ni, vil RAZ-za DAN-NA-ta.' As always, be careful to pronounce clearly both letters when you have a double consonant in Italian. This is especially critical in as dramatic a piece as this, for it will give the line strength and shape:

Andante mosso agitato

Cor - ti - gia - ni,   vil raz - za   dan - na - ta,

"You can take a bit of time when you reach the word 'tesor,' for it needs emphasis ('TE-sor'), if the conductor will permit it. Sometimes it is difficult for an orchestra to hold back in a passage such as this where the notes move very swiftly, and the conductor will wish to keep his players going. But here you must try to persuade him, for 'tesor' needs to be highlighted if possible; it is the value Rigoletto places on his daughter. Give it as much feeling as you can:

"Just before the first climax ('se dei figli difende l'onor'), keep the string of C's ('nulla in terra più l'uomo paventa') bound tightly together and do not slacken the drive:

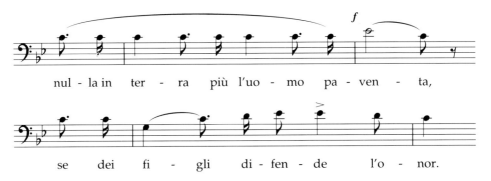

In the final syllables of 'difende' and the first of 'l'onor,' you may alter the line and sing G above the staff rather than the written E-flats:

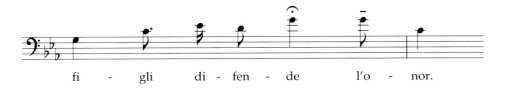

This is another example of 'good' tradition, for it strengthens the climax. Make certain, however, that you attack the G's squarely without slowing down the pace before these high notes.

"After this, you must continue to drive and 'Quella porta, assassini' must run to the E-flat of 'm'aprite.' Be careful not to exaggerate the E-flat, however, by holding it longer than written:

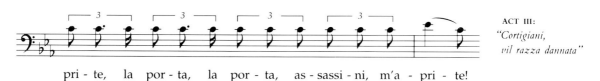

pri - te,   la por - ta,   la por - ta,   as - sassi - ni,   m'a - pri - te!

"The next section ('Ah! voi tutti a me contro') must have great expression, but make your expression on the notes and with supported tone. Give good emphasis to 'TUT-ti' and to 'CON-tro' ['you *all* are *against* me'] and to 'AH! EB-BEN-E PIAN-go' (it is necessary to add the final *e* to 'ebben' to give the line greater emphasis and to push to the word 'piango'):

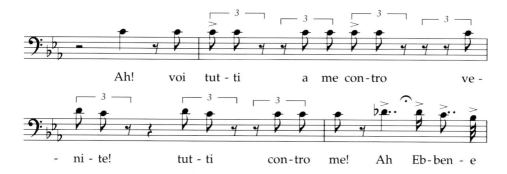

Ah!   voi tut - ti   a me con - tro   ve - ni - te!   tut - ti   con - tro me!   Ah Eb - ben - e

"At this point, Rigoletto, aware that the courtiers are unmoved, narrows his plea to one of them, Marullo. 'Tu ch'hai l'alma gentil come il core' [You, who have a soul as gentle as your heart], he says, trying to move Marullo, gain his help. That must be somewhat exaggerated, for Rigoletto doesn't really believe what he is saying. He says it only because he is desperate; he is crying, but angry that he *must* cry.

"At the end of this section ('è là? non è vero?') do not make a rallentando, but keep the line moving and push it to 'tu taci!' Make the F of 'tu' very short and the F of 'taci' very strong, as though Rigoletto were trying to crush Marullo with the note. Then, ride the F down and really dig into 'OHI-mè!':

è   là?   non è   ve - ro?   è   là?   non è   ve - ro?   tu   ta - ci!   ohi - mè!

"The nice cantabile that follows is very legato and sustained, but underneath it you must make the public feel Rigoletto's bitterness at being on his knees before those who have taken his child. In this section, watch carefully the two short C's in 'pietate' and 'ridate.' The first is an acciaccatura and the second is a sixteenth note. A careful distinction must be made between them:

"Later, at 'Ridonarla a voi nulla ora costa,' attach the '-la' of 'nulla' to the very end of the E-flat or you will spoil the note's effect. Also, give good, strong accents to 'TUT-to, TUT-to al mondo,' because to Rigoletto, Gilda is *all, all the world.* Also, take the 'è' following 'mondo' and put it in after 'figlia.' This will give the line more power, for you can then take a breath after 'mondo' and make a solid attack on 'tal figlia':

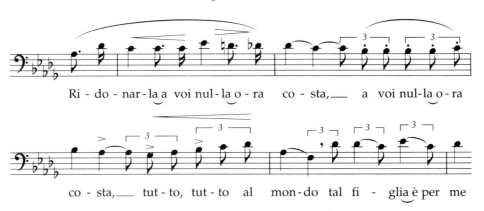

"And when you sing the 'pietà' before 'Ridate a me la figlia,' make a good portamento to 'ridate' and attack the upper note dead center. But when this phrase is repeated, ride the lower F up, but take a quick catch breath before the second top F and make a fresh attack on the upper note. This will give the line more expression and also allow breath for the following phrase, which goes to G-flat. Sing the G-flat in tempo, but pause on the F that follows, accent 'FI-glia' well, and then breathe again:

mon-do è tal fi-glia per   me;— ri-da-te a me— la   fi-glia;

"Before the final unaccompanied phrases, stop and breathe deeply before beginning; do not be in a hurry here. Then breathe again after 'ell'è per me,' to emphasize Rigoletto's deep feelings for his daughter:

In the last phrase, do not linger too long on the high F and do not overdo the rest after 'signori.' Keep the line moving swiftly ahead into the final 'pietà.' Breathe well before the C of 'pietà,' and make the last D-flat full of feeling.

ACT III: *"Tutte le feste . . .*
Piangi, fanciulla . . . Sì, vendetta"

"At the beginning of this scene, Gilda's sound must be penetrating, like a cry; she is in great anguish. Rigoletto, however, is so happy to have his daughter back, he does not realize at first what has happened to her. Verdi has filled his music with rests to break up his phrases, as though he were breathless: 'Signori . . . in essa . . . è tutta la mia famiglia. . . .' To convey this, and because the music is moving swiftly, pronounce well:

Allegro assai vivo ed agitato

Si - gno - ri   in es - sa   è tut - ta la mia fa - mi-glia

"When Gilda tells her father she has been dishonored, the tone must remain full when she drops the octave from F:

Ah! l'on - ta, pa - dre mi - o!

" 'Ite di qua, voi tutti' must have great authority. Rigoletto is like an angry king here, commanding his subjects:

I - te di qua,   voi tut - - ti

"Before beginning 'Tutte le feste,' Gilda should breathe after 'Ciel,' attack the G of 'dammi' cleanly, and the sound must be forward for 'coraggio.' Remember, however, that she says this to herself:

(Ciel!   dam - mi co - rag - - - gio!)

"The aria begins simply. Be careful of the double consonants: 'Tut-te,' 'Id-dio,' 'bel-lo,' 'of-friasi,' 'lab-bri.' These will add color to the line:

Tut - te le fe - ste al tem - pio   men - tre pre - ga - va Id-

- di - o,   bel - lo e fa - ta - le un gio - va - ne

of - fria - si al guar - do mi - o   se i___ lab - bri no - stri

"Gilda's singing should become more open with 'e con ardente palpito,'
and 'amor mi protestò' should be delivered with great enthusiasm. I would
move 'mi' from A to G and breathe just before it; it will be more dramatic
this way:

"Do the same thing with 'm'addussero nel l'ansia'; move the 'nel' to
F-natural and breathe before it. Also, do not slow down on the triplets; move
through them quickly:

Again, I would breathe after 'l'ansia' just before 'più crudel':

"The next section for Rigoletto must move forward relentlessly with sharp
rhythm. The phrases are long here, so when you breathe, make it deep to carry
you through:

"Very important here is the repetition of 'tutto.' Accent each well. Though
the tempo does not stop here, there is a gradual easing of the tension, a sort
of dying away before 'Piangi, fanciulla':

ACT III:
"Tutte le feste"

Ma tut - to,   ma tut - to   o - re scom - pa - re.

"Breathe deeply before the fermata on 'ah,' attack the C well, and make a small portamento into the D-flat. This must be filled with feeling:

(rove) - sciò! Ah!   Pian - gi,   pian - gi, fan - ciul - la, fan-ciul - la,

"I would also breathe before the second 'fanciulla'; it will be more dramatic. When Gilda sings 'Padre!' she should let her voice out, it should be full of anguish. And Rigoletto must give us both of the *r*'s of 'scorrer.' This is very important:

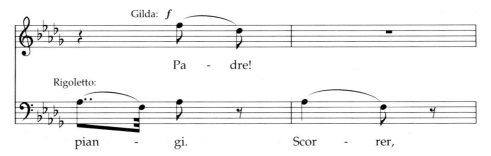

Gilda: *f*

Pa - dre!

Rigoletto:

pian - gi.   Scor - rer,

"The ensemble becomes difficult in the final section of this duet, and it is important that both artists look at one another while singing and be aware of what each is singing. On stage, one must help the other:

p

Gilda: *simile*

(an) - gel,_____ pa - dre, in__ voi_____ par - la un__

Rigoletto:

cor   pian - gi,   pian - gi,

It is especially important in the final five measures that both breathe together, like this:

"Rigoletto should wait until the orchestra has stopped before beginning 'No, vecchio, t'inganni.' Make it strong, and an E-flat can be sung on 'avrai' instead of the last C. I would also ride the E-flat down to begin 'Sì, vendetta.' This stretta needs great power and drive. Rigoletto is furious, but not so furious that the triplets are not clear:

"Gilda's entry must be very impetuous. She is a heroine here, begging for her lover's life:

ACT III:
"Tutte le feste"

O   mi - o   pa - dre,__ qual   gio - ia__ fe -(roce)

"By tradition—and a good one, I think—the più mosso should start a little sooner than it is marked, with Rigoletto's 'Come fulmin scagliato da Dio,' then increase even more where it is marked poco più. The triplets are tricky here for Gilda and later for Rigoletto. You must work them out slowly; they have to be heard:

A   noi__ pu - re il per - do - no dal

"If you like, the ending can be altered to include an E-flat for Gilda and an A-flat for Rigoletto, like this:

(perdo) - na - te, per - do - na - te,__ ah!_____

(col) - pi - re il buf - fo - ne'__ ah! sa - prà._____

VERDI ❧ IL TROVATORE

ACT II: *"Stride la vampa"* and *"Condotta ell'era in ceppi"*

"This aria is very straightforward but very intense. It must be sung as though Azucena were in a trance, yet it needs to have a fierce attitude to it. There are many accents, and each must be heard. Your rhythm as well must be sharp. Begin the trills at once; you cannot afford to lose time on them or you will lose the power of the music as well:

"The words are extremely important here, and more so later. Once you pronounce a word, it must then be sustained with your diaphragm, such as 'cinta di sgherri':

"Be certain to keep the trill in both verses on 'ciel' going for its full time. This is terror, and it must be sustained to have its proper effect:

"Just after 'Stride la vampa,' the two phrases 'Mi vendica' are extremely important; they are really the heart of this drama. Give them importance. There is a diminuendo on the second, but even so, you must keep the tension going underneath:

Mi ven - di - ca! mi ven - di - ca!

" 'Condotta ell'era in ceppi' is much like 'Stride la vampa'—direct and very emotional. Again, when you have a piece as supercharged and dramatic as this, with the horror of a mother who has burned her own child to death, you must lean on the words forcefully. This will carry the drama, spare your voice, and allow the music to project over the orchestra. Don't forget your accents:

Con - dot - ta el - l'e - ra in cep - pi

"The allegretto has been marked by Verdi 'sotto voce e declamato,' which means it must be almost hushed, as though she is frightened to retell this terrible experience; yet the words need underlining with your voice:

Allegretto
sotto voce e declamato

Quan - d'ec - co a - gl'e - gri spir - ti,

"Most of the phrases in this section end with two eighth notes, and nearly every one of them requires a strong accent: 'SPIR-ti,' 'ap-PAR-ve,' 'fe-RA-le,' 'LAR-ve,' and so forth:

(ap) - par - ve (fe) - ra - le lar - ve!

"The A of 'vendica' must be full; don't slight its value. Also, I would leave it by way of a portamento:

"The next part, Verdi wants agitatissimo; the words here must be almost exaggerated. Remember, you have a long way to go, and the phrases must continually build in power and intensity until you reach the high B-flat. Plan this section carefully, and remember that the high note is not just a cry of despair but a B-flat, and it has to have a full sound; let your voice out:

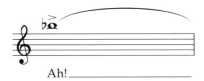

" 'Il figlio mio,' which follows, must be almost hammered out. Lean hard on the consonants so that the sound will continue throughout the phrase:

"After all of this, you still have the most dramatic moment to come, so make certain to save something for it. Full low notes are needed here. Don't forget both *z*'s of 'drizzarsi,' and on the last 'drizzarsi' I would sing all of the word on D-sharp to E rather than to C, so that the C can be given entirely to 'an-.' It makes a more dramatic ending:

ACT II: *"Il balen del suo sorriso"*

"Count di Luna is a nobleman, so there must be authority to your sound. Nearly every phrase of the recitative before 'Il balen' is a different thought, a different attitude. So break it down into its parts so that you can convey these differences. For example, the first, 'Tutto è deserto,' has less importance than what follows. Sing it simply, calmly, but with support. Look about you; show the public you are alone, you see no one. You can't sing this recitative with your eyes on the floor:

Tut-to è de-ser-to;   nè perl'au-re an-co-ra suo-na l'u-sa-to car-me.

"Begin to open up with 'Ardite, e qual furente amore,' and give even more on 'Spento il rival'—here he is gloating that his rival for Leonora is dead. You need a different sound than before; there must be triumph to the voice:

Spen-to il   ri-val,   ca-du-to o-gni o-sta-col sem-bra-va

"As the recitative becomes more intense in its emotion, take time to calculate well your breathing. Di Luna's changing thoughts can be emphasized by how you breathe. Give your breath to the public as an expression of the strength of his feelings. Also, I would move the recitative at 'a' miei desiri.' If you consume too much breath here and on the next few phrases, you will not be sufficiently ready for the two big ones that end the recitative:

più mosso

a' miei de - si-ri;   no-vel-lo e più pos-sen-te el-la ne ap-pre-sta

"The climax comes when di Luna speaks the name of Leonora. Really let your voice blossom here; she is the one he loves. When you sing her name, your face must open—also your throat! On the second 'Leonora' you may raise the line to G-natural; it gives the name more importance:

"The aria itself must be rich, full of love and passion, generous but always rhythmic. Sing as you would play a cello. Play on your voice; this is your instrument. The tempo is largo, but it mustn't be too slow, or you will lose your support and the music will drag:

"Be careful of the gruppetti on 'amore' and 'mio.' Don't lose time here. Sing these notes as if they were six equal notes. Also, you are going to need a breath in 'le favelli in mio favor' in order to give the end of this phrase the importance it deserves. Therefore, I would repeat the E of 'favelli' and sing the second E on 'in,' breathing just before it:

"Again, do not let the aria slow down for 'suo' and 'tempesta'; move right through these notes:

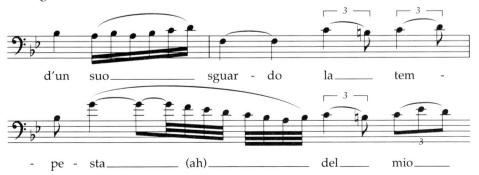

"Verdi asks you to sing 'con espansione' at 'Ah! l'amor, l'amor ond'ardo,' so make these phrases big; give him your voice:

"Just before the cadenza, wait! Don't be in a rush. Prepare yourself well before offering it. A cadenza other than the one in the score is traditionally sung. It is more dramatic, and better, I think. But sing right through it; save yourself for the end. 'Mio cor' is what is important and the place where you should give the most:

VERDI &~ LA TRAVIATA

ACT I: *"Ah! fors'è lui . . . Sempre libera"*

"Violetta, like Norma, has a nobility about her, for she sacrifices herself for love, and both are purified in the end because of their sacrifice. Their music, however, is very different. Both sing great melodies, but Verdi's are more giving. They come to the ear and the mind immediately and stay there. Verdi once said, 'Never mind the quality of a melody as long as it can be recognized even when sung by a shoeshine boy.' And this is the sort of melody you find in *La traviata*—easy, but very intense.

"Actually, it was easier to find a different color for Violetta than the one I used for Norma, because she is a different kind of woman, from a different time and background, and has a different strength. Therefore, you *must* use a different sort of intensity and approach. Violetta is younger, more enthusiastic. In the first act she laughs and says 'Well, let's try.' But in the second act she says 'Let's hope.'

"There are only certain moments in Violetta's music when you should sing out; the rest are mezzo-forte and piano. It takes a long time to learn this, however. When you are young, the tendency is to give and give, especially because you want to please the public, which likes long notes. But with the years, you learn to underplay such things, and the drama then increases.

"Her aria in the first act, 'Ah! fors'è lui,' is Violetta's awakening to real love. As in most recitatives, there are many attitudes here; she is thinking out loud. Her first line, 'È strano' [How strange], is a reflection. It comes after a thought: 'Why do the words of this young man disturb me?'

"Begin 'È strano' right on the dot, and measure carefully the pause after the repeat of these words. There is always a rhythm to a pause; it must be measured inside yourself, so that the pulse of the music will continue even through a rest:

"The next phrase should be sung in tempo, but it needs a slower attitude. Don't rush here. In fact, always take your time to convey a thought, even if the tempo is a quick one:

" 'Oh gioja' is important and must be emphasized by pausing on the B-flat. But when you leave it, come down quickly:

Oh gio - - - ja ch'io non co - nob - bi,

"You must also take time with 'esser amata amando'—'I have never known what it means to love and be loved.' Make a crescendo on the D of 'amata' and accent well 'a-MAN-do':

es - ser a - ma - ta a man - do!

"You may give a little more than is written on the A-flat of 'follie,' for she is asking herself, 'Do I dare dismiss this love for the empty folly of my life?' Do not stretch out 'mio' more than Verdi has done. Sing through these notes to the final C:

l'a - ri-de fol - li - e del vi - ver mi - - - o?

"As I noted earlier, the attitude for 'Ah! fors'è lui' is like that of 'Caro nome': both are inner thoughts, both involve love, and both have a rather halting or breathless quality at first. The difference is that Violetta's second phrase has more love in it; she is, after all, a more experienced woman:

Ah, for - s'è lui che l'a - ni - ma

"In the first section of the aria, it is traditional and effective to pause on the upper A-flat. Make a portamento to and from it—gently, no great scoops—and make the note itself piano:

so - lin - ga ne' tu - mul - ti, so - lin - ga ne' tu - mul - ti,

"Be careful of 'Lui, che modesto e vigile.' It is low and marked pianissimo, and there is a chance you might drop your support here. Don't!:

"On the E of 'amor,' before the aria shifts to F major, ride the E up to an F, breathe well, and then begin 'A quell'amor.' This will increase the intensity of Violetta's feelings, especially if you follow it with a good phrase, full of meaning. Verdi asks that it be sung con espansione:

"Give great importance to 'dell'universo, dell'universo intero'—'This love is my entire universe':

"Put a fermata on the G of 'croce,' then breathe well before continuing:

"The second verse of this aria is too much and should be cut; we've heard all of this once, and that's enough. So on 'cor' jump to three bars before the cadenza.

"You have several possibilities for this cadenza. At first I sang my own, but later I turned to the original. It is by far the best. But you need a breath in the middle of it; I would breathe after you reach the B-flat and have finished your vocalizing, move from E up to D, and breathe again. You can either finish the cadenza as written or continue up to F. I have done it both ways. You make your own choice:

"The next recitative—'Follie!'—must move quickly. Do not let up your momentum when you reach the vocalizing, though you may emphasize the two B-flats of 'gioir' and the D-flat. Also, I would make the first 'gioir' forte, the second piano, then the D-flat forte again:

" 'Sempre libera' must be very brilliant and open. Don't forget the trills; sing right on them:

"The approach to the high C's in this cabaletta is difficult in terms of planning your breathing. It is better if you can get a quick breath before each C, like this:

"Sing all the scales on 'ah,' and make them absolutely even, like oil:

(vo) - lar, dee____ vo - lar (ah)____

"If it is more comfortable for you, sing only the first 'il mio pensier' in the coda. Then, drop out for two and a half measures, and re-enter on the B-flat. If you like, and if you have the note, you may sing an E-flat at the end. This is a bravura piece, so why not? If this note is not comfortable for you, you can sing a B-flat instead:

il____ mio pen - sier, ah, ah____ ah___ sì.

or pen - sier!

ACT IV: *"Addio del passato"*

"This is an aria of great sadness; Violetta is a desperate woman here. Make a portamento from the A to F-sharp of 'attendo,' and accent 'GIUN-gon':

At - ten - do, at - ten - do, nè a me giun-gon ma - i!

Move right through 'Ma il dottore a sperar pure m'esorta,' then accent 'MOR-bo,' make a crescendo on 'morta' and carry the note down to the lower E:

mor - bo   o - gni spe - ran - za è mor - - ta!

"When you begin the aria, don't pull back on the rhythm. Keep it moving. Remember: when you steal time to make a rubato, as you must do on a word like 'ridenti,' you have to give back what you have taken, so that the phrase continues to move:

so - gni___ ri - den - ti, le

"Take time for a deep breath after 'pallenti,' then start the next phrase piano and gradually crescendo. This is a difficult phrase, and if you don't begin it softly, you cannot increase the tension within the phrase as you move forward. Also, by beginning quietly, you'll need only one breath to get you through it:

pal - len - ti; l'a - mo - re d'Al -

- fre - do___ per - fi - no___ mi man - ca,

"Take the B of 'sostegno' up to C-sharp on 'ah,' and then breathe well before 'della traviata':

so - ste - gno. Ah! del - la___ Tra - via - ta___

"The high A of 'Dio' is a problem. It mustn't be too short or too long. It should be like a cry to heaven, but not overdone:

tu ac - co - gli - la, o Di - o!

"The last phrases should also start piano, with a crescendo on the A, and then gradually become less and less intense as you go down. The final A, which Verdi marks 'un fil di voce,' can take a messa di voce, but, again, do not overdo this effect:

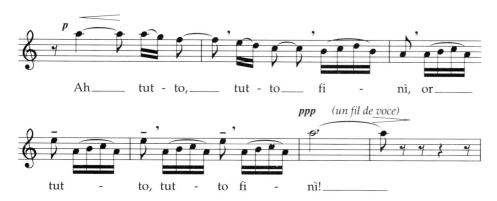

Ah___ tut - to,___ tut - to___ fi - nì, or___

tut - to, tut - to fi - nì!___

"Cut the second verse entirely. It adds nothing; in fact, it would only detract from what you have done.

VERDI ✺ *I VESPRI SICILIANI*

ACT II: *"O tu, Palermo"*

"Remember the situation here: Procida is a great, historic figure, who has just returned from exile to liberate his country from the French. And he is Sicilian on top of it! There must be nobility to every phrase he sings. Feel this nobility —feel big before you begin to sing, put it on your face.

"Take your time with the opening recitative; give us your voice. He is saying, 'Oh my God, I am finally home.' In the theater you should go on your knees as you sing these important words. Make a nice legato drop on the C octave of 'patria,' and accent 'o CA-ra PA-tria, al-FIN, alfin TI veggo':

O pa - tria,   o ca - ra pa - tria,   al-fin, al-fin ti veg-go!

"The only sweetness comes in the andante, 'Il fiorente tuo suolo'; caress it:

Il   fio - ren - te   tuo   suo - lo

"The end of the recitative must be rich in feeling. This is a hero, a proud man, and he is saying, 'I pledge to you my arm and my heart.' I would breathe after 'braccio' so that you can give a good strong emphasis to 'e il core,' but remember, expression consumes breath, so take time through this scene to breathe well; it will also heighten the drama:

re - co il mio_ vo-to a te   col brac - cio e il   co - re!

"The aria should be sung with authority, fullness, love. The acciaccatura is cantabile as well; it mustn't stick out:

O   tu, Pa - ler - mo,   ter - ra a - do - ra - ta,

Breathe after 'riso d'amor,' and it is the C of 'ah' you must hold, not the B-flat:

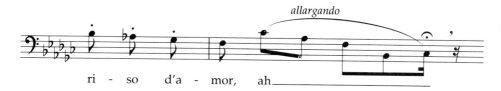

ri - so d'a - mor, ah_____

"Begin giving more with the next phrase. He says, 'Sicily, lift up your head; you have suffered enough.' When you reach 'primier splendor,' it is, each time, 'SPLEN–dor.' Put this in your eyes as well as your throat. Incidentally, I think this passage, 'primier splendor,' should be rearranged a bit, so that you can take a good breath here. Sing it like this:

pri - mier splen - dor,_____ il__ tuo__ ri - (piglia)

"Also, I would breathe between the two 'primier's in the next phrase. Begin the gruppetti at once. If you don't get up to the C quickly, you will run out of breath:

(ri) - pi - glia pri - mier,__ pri - mier_____ splen - dor!

"Beginning with 'Chiesi aita a straniere nazioni,' I would move the tempo more. This will build tension which then will be released when 'O tu, Palermo,' returns:

Chie - si ai - ta a stra - nie - re na - - zio - ni,

"Sing 'a vittoria' very rhythmically and with force. These D-flats are almost like trumpet calls. On the last ('all'onor'), hold the note and make a crescendo on it:

(all'o) - nor!_____   a vit - to - ria,   al - l'o - nor!

"Continue through the balance of the aria as you began it. There is a nice cadenza waiting for you at the end. Move through it quickly; what is important here is not the little notes but the final 'primiero almo splendor,' which must be as big as you can make it. In the very last phrase, I would breathe after 'almo' so that 'splendor' will have more power:

ah_____   tor - na al   pri - mie -

- ro   al - mo splen-dor,   al - mo   splen - dor!

"If the cadenza Verdi has written is not comfortable for you, there is an alternate often heard which you might prefer:

tor-na al pri - mie - ro al-mo splen-dor,   al-mo   splen-dor!

VERDI ❧ SIMON BOCCANEGRA

PROLOGUE: *"Il lacerato spirito"*

"This aria is sung by a man in great anguish, but don't make it too broad. Grief does not mean moaning. He has dignity, so sing with authority and dramatic warmth.

"Watch the double *d*'s of 'addio' and 'freddo'; they will heighten the line. In this case, you may also roll the *r* of 'freddo':

A te l'e-stre-mo ad-di - o, pa-la-gio al-te-ro, fred-do

On the D of 'mio,' let us have your voice; vibrate the sound:

se - pol - cro del-l'an - gio-lo mi - o!

"Sing out, as well, 'E tu, Vergin, soffristi'—Fiesco is crying out against the Virgin:

E tu, Ver - gin, sof-fri - sti

"You will need a big sound here to contrast with the next phrase: immediately after accusing the Virgin, Fiesco is appalled at his words, so 'Ah! che dissi? deliro!' must come as a consequence. It should not be breathless, but hushed and sustained. Never let your sound down in this aria, even at pianissimo:

Ah che dis-si? de - li - ro! ah, mi per - do - na!

" 'Il lacerato spirito' is an expression of deep sadness, yet with power. Your sound must be round and your line sustained. At 'Il serto a lei de' martiri,' move the music more, make it liquid, warm up your sound:

Il   ser - to a lei   de'   mar - ti - ri

"Verdi has marked 'prega, Maria, per me' pianissimo, but remember that the sound has to go from you through the stage and over the orchestra before it reaches the public. It must be well supported and well within your voice. A bass, especially, must put out a bit more sound than others on a pianissimo; it cannot be as delicate an expression as that of a tenor, for example:

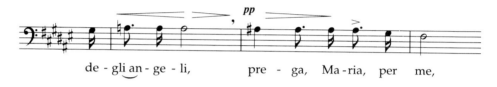

de - gli an - ge - li,   pre - ga, Ma - ria, per   me,

"At the final phrase, breathe before the first C-sharp and after the second. Don't waste time here. Immediately head to your low note; you will then have enough breath to sustain the F-sharp, and the note will come better:

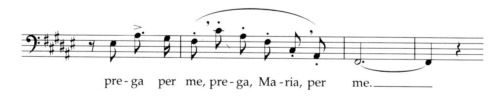

pre - ga   per me, pre - ga, Ma - ria, per   me._____

VERDI ❧ UN BALLO IN MASCHERA

ACT III: *"Eri tu"*

"This aria takes a lot of thought before you can perform it. You must first reduce it to its essentials and have a complete grasp of its moods. Renato is a mature man who has loved and lost his love. At first he reacts with anger, then with great affection. But in both there must be a quality of suffering. Even a young artist must learn how to suffer, be a good actor, live an emotion.

"The tone here must be round and beautiful, not biting. I wouldn't make too much of the opening recitative. Give the notes their value, but no more. I would make an exception, however, of the F-flat. It can take a bit more emphasis. Also, I would breathe after it before going on to 'il tuo rossore':

"Bring the recitative back into tempo at the allegro. Later, be careful of your entrance at 'Altro.' The orchestra ends on an A-sharp, and you must begin with G-natural. Your pitch must be exact to convey the tension Verdi intended here. Also, attack 'ben' cleanly; no sliding:

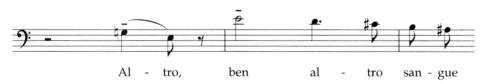

"Don't bang out the notes of the agitato section—'E lo trarrà il pugnale.' Make it always legato, always moving forward:

"The three 'vendicator's at the end of the recitative must be weighted differently. The first comes at the end of a big phrase, so it will be powerful. The second is a little less strong, but still with anger. Don't overdo this, however; remember the human quality of this man—he is not Iago. The final 'vendicator' is less strong still, but darker, somewhat covered in quality. Each time, accent the word 'VEN-di-ca-tor':

"The aria itself should not be sung too forte or too fast. He is reflective here, baring his soul. The thought is from within. Connect the notes well, always legato:

"This cantabile quality continues even when you are more open in expression, such as 'Traditor! che compensi in tal guisa.' The human quality of Renato must continue to be felt here. When I say 'human,' however, I do not mean that you should lose your firmness of tone. The attitude comes in how the tones are tied together:

"In the phrase 'dell'amico tuo primo la fè,' I would make a ritard. Take the turn slowly, hold the B-flat, and let the sound relax as you phrase down to F:

del - l'a - mi - co   tuo   pri - mo   la   fè!

"The second attitude comes from 'O dolcezze perdute!' Renato is remembering how sweet was his love for Amelia, how complete. This section to the end must be very espressivo and deeply felt. When you come to the turns, move quickly through them so that the line continues to flow:

d'un   am - ples - so   che l'es - se - re in - di - a!

I would breathe after 'sul mio seno' to set off 'brillava d'amor':

sul   mio   se - no   bril - la - va   d'a - mor!

After the next 'brillava d'amor' on the high G, breathe after 'd'amor,' then sing the F on 'si':

sul   mio   se - no   bril - la - va   d'a - mor, si   bril - la - va   d'a - mor!

"Put great passion into 'È finita'; then, on 'non siede che l'odio' up to G-flat, broaden the line, breathing after 'l'odio' and 'morte':

ACT III:
"Eri tu"

non sie - de che l'o - dio, che l'o - dio e la

mor - te nel ve - do - vo cor!

"Don't take too much time on the fermata of 'o speranze.' Save your power for the final F, and make a long crescendo on it:

o spe-ran - ze_____ d'a - mor, d'a - mor, d'a - mor!_____

VERDI ✑ *LA FORZA DEL DESTINO*

ACT I: *"Me pellegrina ed orfana"*

"The words of this aria are very explicit. Your job is to put them into your voice. Leonora is giving up everything for Don Alvaro—country, father, family—and she is not exactly happy about it.

"This aria is heavy work, but there is no need to push to be dramatic. Drama comes from clean pronunciation and intensity of expression. Keep your voice free, more towards the lips. Never sing from your throat. There should be no thickness to the sound; it should be pure, open.

"In the recitative, fill 'Io non amarlo' with feeling, then move on quickly.

'Patria, famiglia, padre' should be urgent. Be careful at 'per lui' and later at 'Ahi troppo' not to weigh down the phrase too much:

"With repeated notes such as you find in the aria's first two phrases, there is a tendency to slow down, especially when they are marked for emphasis as Verdi has done here. You must sing through them; keep the line moving:

"The same is true of 'Colmo di tristi immagini.' In fact, here Verdi asks for an accelerando. Accent well 'affranto' in the next phrase:

" 'Di questa misera' is like an outcry, but do not overstay on the G:

"The breathing is very important in the next phrases. If you can, try to go from 'colmo di tristi immagini' through 'da' suoi rimorsi affranto' in a single breath, putting the '-to' of 'affranto' on E before breathing, then singing 'è il' on the C. If this is too much for you, then breathe after 'immagini':

ACT I:
*"Me pellegrina
ed orfana"*

pian - to col - mo di tri - sti im - ma - gi - ni,

crescendo

da' suoi ri - mor - si af - fran - to è il cor di

"Make a ritard on the B-flat, but sing 'dannato a eterno pianto' in tempo. Emphasize 'PIAN-to' and phrase the D-flat to the C:

dan-na-to al pian - to,____ dan-na-to a e-ter-no pian - to.

"The next section is like sighs of sadness and goes in and out of tempo. Begin strictly, but make an allargando with the high F. Each time you have 'addio,' give it deep feeling:

Ti la - scio, ahi-mè,__ ahi-mè, con la - cri - me, dol -

- ce mia ter - ra!   ad - di - o.

"Sing the next 'Ti lascio, ahimè' with passion but without slowing down the tempo; be exact rhythmically:

Ti   la - scio, ahi - mè, con   la - cri - me,

"The line will be better if you sing 'o dolce mia terra' instead of simply 'dolce mia terra':

"At 'Per me,' be certain to sing D-natural and not D-sharp:

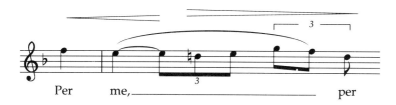

"Again, I would like 'per me non avrà termin' when it appears the second and third times to be a single phrase. You can also sing 'sì gran dolor, sì gran dolor' in one phrase as well, if you do not waste too much breath on the high A:

"Do not hold the C of 'addio' just before the B-flat too long, or you will not have breath for the top note:

"The final 'addio' should be more intense or less intense than the 'addio' before it. Whichever you choose, be certain the two are different in color:

ACT II: *"Madre, pietosa Vergine"*

"In this scene Leonora is in great agony. She has witnessed the killing of her father by her lover Alvaro and been cursed by her brother. She now seeks refuge in a monastery.

"This is a very tense scene, and Verdi has written a good deal of it in the middle and lower voice. Such passages, especially at the point between the two registers, are difficult for a soprano, so be certain you sustain your sound well throughout.

"Begin with a good accent: 'Son GIUN-ta!' You can sing 'grazie, o Dio' and subsequent low-lying passages in chest voice if you like, but if you do, make certain they are well supported, in the mask, or the orchestra will cover you. Also, a phrase such as 'Estremo asil quest'è per me' will be lost unless you sing on the word, pronouncing well:

"Give 'Io tremo!' and 'La mia orrenda storia' drive. These should be sung with fear in the voice. It is 'TRE-mo' and 'or-REN-da':

"Move quickly to 'Se scoperta m'avesse!' She is saying 'What if someone should find me?'; she is frightened:

(nar)- rol - la!   Se sco-per - ta m'a - ves - se!

"In the next phrase accent well 'NA-vi-ga' and 'Al-VA-ro':

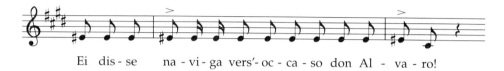

Ei dis - se   na - vi - ga vers'- oc - ca - so don Al - va - ro!

"Give emphasis, too, to 'Io' both times it occurs:

cad - de   quel-la not - te in cui   i - o,   i - o

"Let out your voice at 'del sangue di mio padre intrisa,' accenting strongly 'DI MIO PADRE':

del san - gue di mio pa-dre in - tri - sa,

"With 'Ed or mi lascia,' the attitude changes. Before, Leonora was consumed with terror; here, she is afraid God has abandoned her. Vibrate your sound well, and build these two phrases so that the top B comes as a natural consequence:

Ed   or   mi   la - scia,

"Phrase down on 'reggo,' 'tan-' and 't'ambascia'; make them like tears:

"The aria is a desperate prayer; Verdi calls it a 'lamento.' It must have great intensity of feeling. Sing well on the notes and with good vowel sounds: '*Mah*-dre.' Work out carefully the crescendo on 'Madre, pietosa Vergine,' and later on 'perdona al mio peccato.' Such expressive details must first be in your mind before they can be in your voice:

"When you reach the two phrases 'pietà di me,' 'pietà, Signor,' attack 'pietà' well and then diminuendo:

Then, with the next 'pietà's, make a crescendo to the half note on D. Put the fermata here rather than on the B, and make a portamento from D to B, then carry the note down to F-sharp and breathe well. You must take time before beginning 'deh! non m'abbandonar'; the air must be clear of the preceding tension:

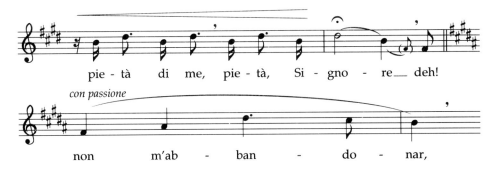

"In this passionate phrase, breathe after the first 'pietà' and again after 'm'abbandonar' before the top A. At the conclusion of the phrase change the words to 'pietà di me, pietà, Signor,' to conform to the sentence as it occurs elsewhere in the aria:

"' 'Ah! que' sublimi cantici' should be sung with great simplicity. Begin to let your voice out more with 'dell'organo i concenti'; here, she becomes inspired by the chanting. In this and the following passages with the chorus, do not fall behind in your rhythm. The chorus is offstage and cannot wait for you; you must find your expression and freedom within their rhythm:

"Bring good emotion to 'inspirano' and later to 'calma':

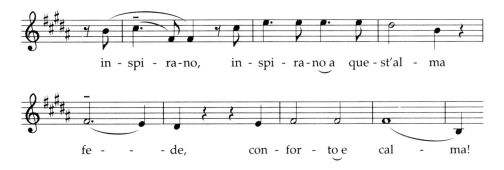

"The declamando is actually a recitative within the aria. There are three different attitudes here. First she says that this sacred refuge will be her home;

then she changes immediately—'But dare I disturb them at this hour?' Finally she asks, 'But what if someone recognizes me here?' As you can see, she is torn by fright and indecision. Put all of this into your voice. Also, the words are difficult to pronounce here, so work them out slowly, get them clean and clear:

"Prepare yourself well for the big crescendo on 'Il pio frate accoglierti.' Make certain you do not drop under pitch with these repeated E's. Keep them moving ahead to the E-sharp, 'no.' Breathe before and after this note, and make a crescendo on the F-sharp. Bring this last 'no' down an octave, barely touching the lower F-sharp. Again, take time to breathe well, then begin 'Non mi lasciar' resolutely; Verdi says 'con più forza'—with more force:

"Each time you have the phrase up to A, breathe after the B, then sing D-sharp, A-sharp, and G-sharp on 'ah':

"The final phrases are a relaxation of the tension that has gone before. Though they are marked piano, make certain they are well supported. On the very last, take a breath before 'Signor' to emphasize this word:

ACT III: *"O tu che in seno agli angeli"*

"Sing the opening, 'La vita è inferno all'infelice,' as it is written, with no exaggeration. It is, after all, a recitative, not an aria. Find a dramatic proportion for the words that is comfortable for you. This will vary with the individual; it is up to you to find what is right in your case. Recitative should be like speech on tones. Verdi has written here long and short notes, but this does not mean that the recitative should be delivered 'La VI-ta è in-FER-no all'-IN-fe-LI-ce.' This would be too mechanical. Speak the line to yourself, and see where the accents would fall naturally.

"For me, it would be 'La vita è in-FER-no all'in-fe-LI-ce,' and this is how I would sing it. Sing through the less important notes to reach the important syllables, then highlight them with your voice. Remember, the recitative is a thought you give the public; it is the statement of an idea that is elaborated on in the aria. Therefore, an aria will have the greater importance, but it is the recitative that prepares the audience for what will follow.

"Be careful on 'desio' not to lose the low notes. Top notes are nice, but the bottom ones are just as important. You will always have the low tones you need if you lean on the words. Also, if you are tired and must sing, the words will help support you:

ACT III:
*"O tu che in
seno agli angeli"*

La vi - ta è in - fer - no al-l'in - fe - li - ce.

In - va - no   mor - te   de - si - o!

"With 'Siviglia' we have a different mood. This is remembrance, hap-
pier days. Caress it. More important, in fact the most important moment
of the recitative, is 'Leonora.' This is the one woman he loved, and he now
believes that she is dead. When he says her name it must be like the world
opening up:

Si - vi - glia!   Leo - no - ra!

"Do not oversing 'Oh, notte ch'ogni ben'; keep it rhythmic. More important is 'mi rapisti.' Even though this is marked dolce, you must give here: 'MI
ra-PI-sti.'

Oh,   not - te ch'o - gni ben   mi ra - pi -   - sti!

"Give, too, on 'Sarò infelice eternamente,' then sing 'è scritto' with calm-
ness, with resignation. This is a key to his thoughts. He is a fatalist; he believes
destiny has written his story:

Sa-rò in - fe - li - ce e - ter - na-men-te   è scrit-to.

ACT III:
*"O tu che in
seno agli angeli"*

"The allegro moderato should be begun simply; it is almost like conversation. He is giving us the history of his family. Gradually, however, you can intensify the sound as you build up to 'sognarono un trono,' the climax of this section:

"Take time for the effect of the high note to dissolve before beginning 'e li destò la scure!' then accent 'SCU-re':

"On the turn of 'sventure,' make the pitches clean and lead the line to the A-flat:

"There should be sadness to the beginning of the aria, so don't give too much here. He imagines Leonora among the angels, forever lost to him:

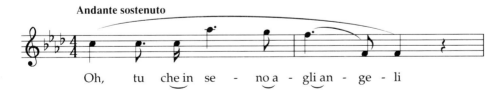

Gradually make a crescendo on 'salisti bella e pura,' then breathe deeply and do not begin 'non iscordar di volger' until you have your breath and are ready to convey the 'dolore' Verdi asks of you:

ACT III:
"O tu che in
seno agli angeli"

"Do not slow down the aria after the first B-flat. Keep the sixteenth notes moving:

"The next phrase is a passionate one; again he invokes Leonora's name. Warm up the phrase with your voice and a portamento:

Take time with the gruppetti on 'soccorrimi'; sing them cleanly:

"On the next B-flat, do not give too much tenuto, for there is another to come which is more important. You can't hold them equally long; you will spoil the effect of the note. Before the final B-flat, don't waste time on the sixteenths. You are only passing through on your way up:

ACT III:
*"O tu che in
seno agli angeli"*

"I would sing the last phrase in one breath if possible. If this is not comfortable for you, breathe after 'pietà,' then continue 'di me':

VERDI ☙ *DON CARLO*

ACT I: *"Nei giardin del bello"*

"This aria must have grace and contrast. If you don't give the music light colors, Eboli will become Amneris. Remember, she is Spanish, noble and beautiful. Perfume the music, sing through the notes, think of her attitude; otherwise the music will become vocalizing, and there is more to it than that.

"Begin the first phrase with *spirito*, animated, but not with too much power or it will be harsh. I know Verdi has marked the opening marcate, but this you must achieve with the words, not your voice. The second phrase must be pianissimo but still well supported:

"When you reach 'tutta chiusa in vel,' play with the notes—start piano, let the phrase grow, and then bring it back to piano:

tut - ta chiu - - - - sa in vel,

"The same is true of 'una stella in ciel,' which follows.

"The first big moment of the aria comes at 'Mohammed, Re moro.' You can be *generosa* with your voice here, but this section will be effective only if you have carefully planned what goes before:

Mo - ham - med,___ Re mo - ro, al giar - din___

"On 'se'n va,' which is actually a slow trill, breathe after the first B and make a small crescendo-decrescendo here, leading your crescendo to the accented A-sharp:

se'n va (ah)___

"Watch well your pitches in 'Vien, a sè t'invita.' You move down by half steps. Verdi has marked this section parlato, and he means that it is almost like speech, except that it is on precise pitches:

Vien, a sè t'in - vi - ta per re - gna - re il Re;

"The cadenza is yours to play with; the orchestra will wait. Make it elegant, but give it mystery as well. The first part, the arpeggios down from G, can gradually increase in speed. Breathe before the first A, and let these repeated A's little by little fade away. I would sing them legato rather than staccato, or you might use a mixture of the two. Whichever you choose, do not scoop up to any of the A's. The final groups of four should be like a murmur which finally dies away. These eight groups of notes must be animated. They cannot all be the same or they will become monotonous:

"Breathe well before starting 'Ah! Tessete i veli,' and you can portamento from the E to the D of 'Ah! Tessete.' Be sure to observe the portamenti Verdi has placed on 'veli,' portamenti that occur at the end of each of the four phrases of this allegro giusto:

"The second verse follows along in the same mood as the first, except at the conclusion there is a scale up to high A. As it is the climax of this aria, I would hold the last note at least a full measure rather than the quarter that is written:

ACT III: *"Ella giammai m'amò"*

"Though this is an intimate piece, one of great suffering, never forget that this is a king who is suffering. He may feel inside the same as ordinary human beings, but he is different. There must always be dignity, regality to his singing. With a king, everything is bigger, more important, and has greater authority. Besides, Philip is also a bass, and a bass's piano is not the piano of another singer. So don't be afraid of giving your voice here; you must.

"The aria begins as though the king were in a trance. There must be intensity to the sound; it must be well vibrated. With repeated notes such as the B-flats in the opening phrases, there will be a tendency to slow the music down. Watch this. Also pronounce well the two *l*'s of 'ella' and the two *m*'s of 'giammai.' Both are crucial to the line. Also be careful of 'chiuso.' We must hear both the *i* and the *u* of 'chi-u-so':

Fill the C-sharp of 'amor' with feeling, and you can give more time than is written to the F-sharp of 'me.' This is the conclusion of a thought and it needs emphasis:

" 'Bianco il dì che qui di Francia' is difficult. Verdi has written staccati under a legato. I had the same problem to solve when I sang Lady Macbeth. What you must do here is emphasize each note within a legato, without weighing down the line:

"Do not overdo the E of 'amor,' but again the F-sharp on 'me' can be held:

No, a - mor per me— non ha! A - mor per me non ha!

"At the end of this phrase, the attitude changes. Before, Philip has been talking to himself. Now he speaks out more, as though awakening from a bad dream:

O - ve son? Quei dop-pier pres-so a fi - nir!

"At the più animato, do not stress all the vowels of 'miei.' It will only slow down your line. Watch your pitches at 'sparì da' miei occhi languenti'; they must be clean. You must breathe just before 'languenti' so that you will be well prepared for this long phrase. Make 'languenti' very decisive, and should you feel yourself running short of air at the end of the phrase, vibrate your sound more so that the audience will not know you have reached the end of your breath.

"Each note of 'languenti' must be well accented. This phrase is typical of Verdi. You will find the same figure just before the beginning of 'Ah! fors'è lui' in *Traviata* and before 'D'amor sull'ali rosee' in *Trovatore*:

Pas - sar veg-go i miei gior - ni len - ti! il son - no, o

Dio, spa - rì da' miei oc - chi lan - guen - - - ti.

"The aria's next section, 'Dormirò sol,' is very serious in mood, and your sound should be round and sure. Make this section very legato and keep it well supported throughout:

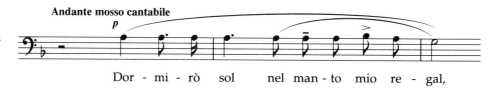

"You must think of the phrase 'dormirò sotto la vôlta nera,' which rises to D, as one big legato. Be generous with your voice here. Just afterwards, take a bit more time with 'là nell'avello' to lead you into the fermata:

"The next section is very dramatic, and the vocalizing here must be very precise:

After leaving the D-flat, take a good breath after 'cor' before going on to 'che Dio sol può veder':

"Though Verdi marks the next section piano, remember this is the king speaking, and what he is saying is too important to be lost: 'If the prince sleeps, the traitor watches; the king loses his crown, the husband loses his honor':

Se dorme il pren - ce, ve - glia il tra - di - to - re;

"At the climax of the aria on D, let us have sound but not too much of the *r* of 'cor.' Keep to the vowel. Take all the time you need to clear the air before the reprise of 'Ella giammai m'amò.' If you rush this, you will not create a sufficient contrast to the outburst just before:

di leg - ge - re nei cor!___ El - la giammai m'a - mò!

"You'll need another good breath just before the final phrase, so that you can give it full importance. The half note on 'ha' need not be held its full value. Take a little from it so that you can breathe properly. Make the concluding phrase very strong. You need not hold the last D longer than is written. It is not the length of a note that determines its importance, but rather the authority with which it is sung:

a - mor per me__ non ha, a - mor per me non ha!

ACT IV: *"Tu che le vanità"*

"Here are the thoughts of a great lady who feels that for her, all is finished. There is sadness here, but always great dignity.

"This scene is very long and contains many different attitudes. It is crucial throughout that you take time to breathe well. This will not only add to the expressiveness of your singing but will make the scene more expansive.

"At the beginning Verdi tells you 'larga la frase'—big phrases. So not only do you need great breath here, but you must be very rhythmic as well, so that phrases move and you do not run out of air. I would carry the upper G-sharp of 'riposo' down to the lower G-sharp not with a portamento—this would make it too broad—but with a good legato. Also, there must be full, firm low notes on the C-sharp of 'mondo' and elsewhere. I would save full chest voice for later in the aria, but 'mondo' can have chest mixed into it. But without a good sound here, there will be no foundation to the scene:

"After this opening declamato, we enter into Elisabetta's private thoughts. First come two matched phrases which must be contrasted. I would sing the first rather fully and begin the second much more softly. However, the second phrase must then build, because you cannot express 'mio dolore' [my sorrow] with a piano sound:

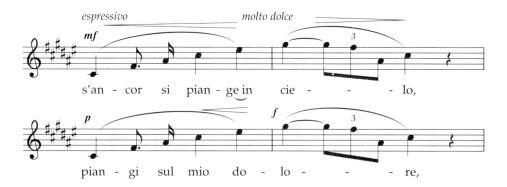

In the next phrase, sing 'mio' entirely on the C-sharp so that you can take a breath before 'al' for the long phrase ahead. In 'trono,' give the accent on the D-sharp Verdi asks of you, and phrase down to the C-sharp that follows. And don't forget the marcate on 'DEL SI-gnor':

The phrase that follows is marked grandioso and should be full in sound. I would even stretch the A just a bit, and then breathe after it before 'porta al trono' so that you can finish this section of aria in a single breath:

"With the allegro there is a change of attitude; Elisabetta anticipates her final meeting with Carlo. This is recitative and must be very rhythmic so that the passage holds together. Accent well 'CAR-lo,' and remember both *r*'s in 'verrà':

Also be careful not to throw away 'Si!' It is important and should be full in sound.

"The allegro moderato which comes next must have great contrast. I would move 'Ei segua il suo destin' [He follows his destiny] quickly, and then pull back on 'Per me, la mia giornata a sera è giunta già!'—'For me, all is finished':

"Still another attitude comes next: She reviews her life, remembering first her childhood in France. This section is all a dream, so do not give it undue importance except for the word 'Francia,' which must be very expressive:

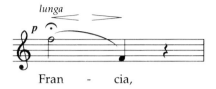

The rest, however, should be simple, unaffected; it is nostalgia. Let your voice out only at the end with 'e quest'eternità un giorno sol durò'—'This eternal love lasted only a day':

"The next section, largo, is also a memory, but it is a bit more giving; it is a memory of her and Carlo's love. In the first phrase, I would ignore the staccati on 'Tra voi, vaghi giardin.' To me, this should be very smooth:

You must observe Verdi's pianissimo on 'che le zolle,' however, for two reasons: You will need to conserve yourself for the crescendo to A-flat, and if the first phrase is too loud, the crescendo will have no effect. Build the crescendo by adding a bit more pressure with each thought: 'i fonti, I BO-schi, I FIOR':

"The agitato which follows is not verismo; you must sing the notes as written. If Verdi had wanted you to do without the notes here, he would have marked this next section parlato. I know it is difficult; it lies in an odd part of the voice, so diction will be of critical importance in realizing this section. Lean on the words, but be careful not to hang on to the end of the phrases where you have eighth notes, such as on 'addio,' 'perduta' and, later, 'muta.' Not only will it weigh down the music if you overdo these notes, but you will deny yourself the opportunity of breathing as well as you must to carry this section:

    ad - di - o,   bei   so - gni   d'ôr,

At 'Il nodo si spezzò, la luce è fatta muta' [The knot is cut, the light is put out] Elisabetta becomes more frantic, but again it is an agitato with control. Never forget she is a queen. In this section you must watch well your pitches —the D-naturals to C-sharp to B-sharp. This must be clean:

  Il no - do si spez - zò, la___ lu - ce, la lu - ce___ è fat - ta

Another phrase that may give you pitch problems unless you are careful is the descending line on 'cedendo al duol crudel.' This must be very legato:

      ce - den - do al   duol   cru - del,

When you reach 'il cor ha un sol desir,' broaden the line, accenting it as Verdi directs, but do not hold on to the E of 'desir.' Cutting it off to the length written in the score will be more dramatic and will tell the public a more important phrase is coming up—'la pace dell'avel' [the peace of the grave]. Breathe well before starting this phrase, then take your time with it. Verdi tells the orchestra to wait for you. Here is where I would use full chest voice:

ACT IV:
"Tu che le vanità"

il   cor ha un sol de - sir: la pa - ce del-l'a - vel!

"The return to 'Tu che le vanità' must be very decisive but very legato. Again, take time to breathe deeply before 's'ancor si piange,' which means you must get off of the C-sharp just before it:

il   ri - po - - - so   pro - fon - do,

"Do not overdo the high A of 'mio' because the high A-sharp that comes a few bars later is more important. This can be held a bit longer than is written because the orchestra will finish before you do, and also because you need to breathe after 'trono' before 'del Signor.' You are still alone at 'se ancor si piange' and 'si piange in cielo,' so do not rush.

"Take your time to give these phrases fully and expressively:

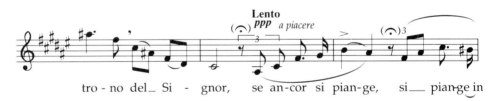

tro - no del_ Si - gnor,   se an-cor si pian-ge,   si_ pian-ge in

"And do not rush into the A of 'ah il pianto mio,' because this phrase must be in a single breath and you must prepare it well:

cie - lo,   ah il pian - to mi - o

"In the last phrase, I would breathe after 'piè' so that 'del Signor' will have greater emphasis. These are the final words of the aria and must have importance. Also save some breath for a final crescendo on the last F-sharp:

re - ca a' piè del Si - gnor._____

VERDI ∽ AIDA

ACT IV: *"L'abborrita rivale"*

"I will deal only with the music for Amneris in this lengthy scene. She is desperate, doing everything in her power to save the life of Radamès, whom she loves. But no matter what the expression—and actually, there aren't that many—remember that Amneris is a princess; her blood is royal. Therefore, when she begs, it is not as an ordinary person would beg; there is grandeur to it.

"Also, in this scene, you must not give, give, give all the time. It will become boring to the public and tiring for you. You must plan colors and contrasts which will allow you to go through the entire scene without exhausting yourself and still remain fascinating to an audience. You must not forget that some of Amneris's most strenuous singing comes at the very end of this long piece of music. So think, plan, and then sing.

"Maestro Serafin once said to me, 'There comes a point when you must forget your studies, forget that there are difficult phrases, difficult high notes. You must let yourself go and love the music, love your phrases, feel your words.' If you are excited, but in control, you will breathe life into your scores, and music will become a living thing. This is what any musician must always strive for.

"Throughout this scene, it is essential that the words be clear and your sound well sustained. Remember, any expression must first be in your mind before you can put it in your voice. In the first phrase, watch the double consonants, and it is 'L'ab-bor-RI-ta ri-VA-!e':

Allegro agitato

L'ab-bor - ri - ta   ri - va - le a me   sfug - gi - a.

" 'Traditor egli non è' must be very impulsive, like the agitato which follows and which shows Amneris's troubled state of mind. Here, and until you reach the first cantabile, measure the notes precisely so that the music keeps moving. Do not lose time, for example, with 'Traditori tutti! a morte! a morte!' but sing right through these notes, pointing the line to the top A-flat:

"She is upset here because she knows Radamès tried to run away with Aida. But suddenly she stops and asks herself, 'What am I saying? I love him.' 'Oh! che mai parlo?' must have great feeling and can be stretched a bit, not only because of the sentiment but because it is the conclusion of the first section of the scene:

"You must be generous with your voice in the next section. 'Io l'amo, io l'amo sempre'—'I love him always, desperately, insanely.' These are strong words, deeply felt. You must put them in your throat:

"At the end of this section she asks herself, 'But how can I save him?' Take advantage of the lungo silenzio Verdi marks in the score. Amneris is struggling in her mind to find a way out for the man she loves. And when she says 'Radamès qui venga,' make it full of authority; this is an order she is giving to the guard to bring Radamès before her:

"Sing 'Già i sacerdoti adunansi' with regality. There is passion to the line, but there is also self-control. Later, she will give way to desperation. Give Verdi the portamento he asks for at 'e nunzia di perdono,' and add another on 'sarò' from C-sharp to F-sharp. Also, this C-sharp must be full in sound; don't let your voice drop out here:

"When Radamès tells her he only wants to die, cut in on him with 'Morire!' You must show that you think it a terrible thing to wish to die. Make the first G-flat of 'Morire' very short so that you can crescendo on the second; it also saves breath and is more effective. Portamento down to the A-flat, then back up to the D-flat. Both of these portamenti are traditional and very effective if done well and with great feeling. This is, after all, a very passionate moment. However, the second portamento should come at the very last moment before you are ready to begin the next phrase:

"You can really let yourself go with 'Ah! tu dei vivere!' It would be well when you are preparing this section to speak the words first. Ask yourself how you would tell someone, 'My God! Live! Live for me!' This is not Medea saying 'I hate you,' it is a woman full of love who wants only to give that love to someone else. Sing these phrases with a rich legato and accent well 'vi-VRA-i,' rolling the *r* if you wish:

"In the next section I would phrase 'orribili' and 'di morte' in twos and dig into 'pro-VA-i':

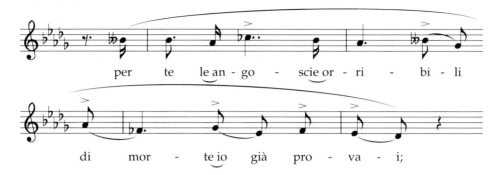

Warm up the next phrase—'t'amai, soffersi TAN-to,' 'I loved you, I suffered for you.' Put feeling into it:

And when you reach 'e patria, e trono,' which Verdi marks grandioso, it should be sung with the greatest joy; you are offering the world to him—Egypt, the throne, your life. Incidentally, on the G-flat to F on 'trono, e,' I would sing '-no' on G-flat, breathe, and then sing 'e' on F, like this:

"Do not hang on to the eighth note of 'vita'; you need a full breath to get past the A-flat that comes up next:

"If your conductor will allow it—and you must ask him very nicely—I would speed up at 'tutto, tutto darei,' and on the fermata give back the time you took. She is saying she will give up everything for him, and it should be impetuous:

tut - to, tut - to da - rei per te.

"At the end of Radamès's next solo, he accuses Amneris of having taken Aida's life. Remember when you answer this that you are a princess who will one day be a queen. Sing 'Io . . . di sua morte origine!' with authority. Draw yourself to your full height and match your phrases to it. Do not lose the acciaccatura on 'Aida.' This is for accent, and I think there should be a cutting sound in your voice when you say 'No! vive Aida,' as if to say 'How dare you accuse me!':

Io di - sua mor - te o - ri - gi - ne!

Più mosso

No! vi - ve A - - - i - da.

"The next section lies low. Sing well on the words, do not rush, and watch your pitches. Later, at 'Ma s'io ti salvo,' be very austere. She has control over herself again, and this and the following phrases must have dignity. She is offering life to him, but now on her terms—'I will save you if you swear never to see her again.' Really give in the next agitato, but still with composure. She is saying 'Who will save you if I do not?' The line must drive to the top B-flat. In this climactic phrase, I would breathe just before 'or dal ciel' and again after the A-flat. You can make the B-flat a bit longer than is written if this is a good note for you. Don't overdo it, but you are on your own here; the orchestra has to wait. The same is true when the phrase is repeated a second time:

ven - det - ta or dal ciel,_____ or__ dal__

"At the end of the duet, breathe just before the F-sharp of 'si.' You will need plenty of breath here not only for the crescendo you must make with the tenor on the G, but because he will probably, I'm sorry to say, scream his head off. This is not very elegantly put, but it is all too true:

Amneris: or_____ dal ciel si com - pi - rà.

Radamès: te - mo, te - mo sol la tua pie - tà.

VERDI ❧ OTELLO

ACT II: *"Credo"*

"It is crucial that the recitative here be as strong as the aria. You have to set the evil of Iago from the very beginning. So start powerfully—'VAN-ne.' Make these two notes separate, and make the sound *ah* less round, a bit more pointed than usual. It should not be a pretty sound; Iago isn't this sort of character:

Van - ne;   la tua me - ta già ve - do.

"After this intense beginning there could be a tendency to let up at 'e il tuo dimon son io.' Don't! The tension in this aria almost never relaxes. Sing this phrase in time, and accent well 'I-o':

e il tuo di - mon son i - o,

"Plan the row of B-flats—'e me trascina il mio, nel quale io credo inesorato Iddio'—so that each one is stronger than the one before. They must become more burning and more marcato, leading you inevitably to the D-flat:

"Really let your voice out with the opening of the aria; give the full sinister nature of Iago, who is really a male Lady Macbeth:

"At 'Dalla viltà d'un germe,' don't change your expression just because the notes are lower. The whole darkness of the character must be felt throughout. When the notes drop, underplay your legato, so it does not interfere with the power of the piece:

"The two phrases up to E-flat must be rhythmic. They are important, but not as important as the C's—'quest'è la mia fè'—that end this section. Stress the C's well; they are like a *giuramento*—an oath. And do not slur down from the last C to the lower F. Remember, in a powerful phrase, whether it is Beethoven or Verdi, you must sing the notes precisely, otherwise you weaken it:

"Begin the next section rather savagely, because you must immediately make a contrast. He says here, 'I believe with all my heart just like the widow in church believes.' So the first part is raw, while the second, marked pianissimo (but not too pianissimo—remember the character!), is calmer, with irony. Stress the words in both, but there is less tension in the second part:

You pick up the tension again with 'che il mal ch'io penso.' Sing right through these notes; don't lose your momentum:

And sing the final C of 'adempio' as written, no more:

The section that follows is like the opening, and again, it should be very rhythmic. The same is true for 'che tutto è in lui bugiardo.' And it is 'BA-cio, SGUAR-do':

"Do not overdo the E-flats of 'sacrificio.' The aria does not stop here but rather is building to a higher point. Begin to move the line more at 'E credo l'uom gioco d'iniqua sorte,' pushing the line to the F-sharp. Come down from this note in strict time; it will be far more dramatic if you do not stretch the line:

"Make 'al verme dell'avel' as stark as possible, even hollow:

"Do not let down your tension in the poco più lento; if anything, this is Iago at his most evil. Keep it dark, and don't throw away 'E poi?' These two questions must have strength, must be frightening. I know that 'La morte è il nulla' is frequently spoken, but I think the effect is less than when you sing the notes as Verdi has written them. Had he wanted them parlato, it would be in the score:

"The last phrase should begin very secco, and when you get to the high F, keep the sound vibrating and increase it in the end. If you generate enough tension here you will not need the laugh many add:

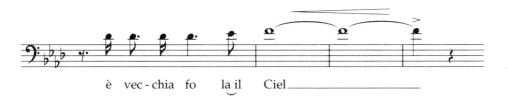

ACT IV: *Willow Song*

"This aria comes after a terrible encounter in the preceding act between Desdemona and Otello. She is sad, uneasy, and fears the worst, for she has had a presentiment of her death. The mood of the aria must be eerie to prepare the audience for her murder. Doing this is not a question of the amount of sound you use—though Desdemona should have a *Pirata* voice—but rather the way you approach this scene. The sound must have an unnatural color, a sense of tragedy.

"Begin frankly, with clean pitches. Don't pick at the repeated notes in the first phrase; keep them legato:

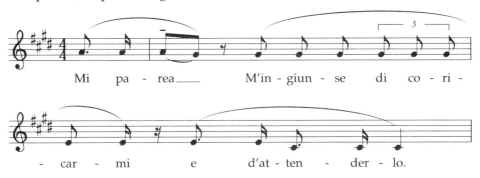

"You especially need a big legato for 'distendi sul mio letto . . . ,' when she tells Emilia to lay her wedding dress out on the bed:

In the next sentence she says, 'If I die before you, let me be shrouded in this dress.' Neither phrase can be sung with just a pretty sound; we must hear unhappiness in both.

"Take your time with 'Son mesta tanto.' Let it be broad; it is the conclusion of the first attitude of the scene:

" 'Mia madre aveva una povera ancella' is recitative. Sing it simply, make it like speech. Desdemona is recalling a girl named Barbara who served her mother, and who also lost her love. In other words, Desdemona is identifying herself with the girl's unhappiness. Because of this, she sings a song Barbara sang, the Willow Song.

"Watch the phrase 'Io questa sera' just before the aria. Do not begin it too piano; it must build to the A-sharp of 'cantilena' before you diminuendo. Also, I would breathe before 'piena.' Make it a deep breath, then give Verdi the stringendo he asks for so that you can carry the phrase through in a single breath:

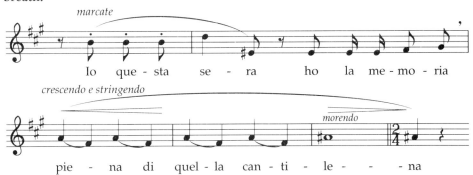

"The aria itself must come from deep within you, it must send shivers up the public's spine. Be careful not to sing the opening 'Piangea' too loudly. Automatically, as a phrase goes up, it becomes loud. Think of this when you plan these notes. If you don't, the phrase will be too heavy, and you will miss the atmosphere so important here:

"Three cries of 'Salce' occur at four different points in the aria. Each 'Salce' needs a different color, and each group must be different from the previous group. For the first time, I would sing the 'salce' forte, then piano, then pianissimo, each time draining a bit more color and vibrancy from your tone until the last is like an echo from a great distance. How you plan the other groups is up to you. The second might begin piano and become louder, the third might be a mixture of the first two, and so forth.

"The important thing is that they have contrast. It is essential here that your attack on each be as clean as possible and your pitch exact. It is very easy to sing under the note here, as there is no orchestra with you; and there is a tendency you might guard against of letting your support drop as you sing more and more piano:

"Be sure to contrast the two 'cantiamo's which follow. The first can be generous, but the second then must be less so:

"Throughout this Willow Song, Desdemona interrupts to speak to Emilia. These breaks must be different than the song itself. For example, when she says 'Affrettati; fra poco giunge Otello' [Hurry up; Otello will soon be coming], this is an order. It should be more or less matter-of-fact:

"A page later, Desdemona interrupts her song again with another order to Emilia. This and the next two phrases should be more open and giving, especially 'Povera Barbara':

"She has barely begun her song again when the sound of the wind terrifies her. She is nervous and upset, and all of this must be in your voice. She continues her song once again; it is finished before the first 'Emilia, addio.' Keep her final lines to Emilia simple until the very end: she is calling her friend back for a last farewell, because she senses she will never see Emilia again. This outburst must be as poignant as possible and should be sung with the same sort of drive a baritone would use in Rigoletto's music:

BERLIOZ ✥ LA DAMNATION DE FAUST

PART IV: *"D'amour l'ardente flamme"*

"This scene must begin from within. These are Marguerite's thoughts, so do not exteriorize too much. The words are passionate, but in those times, and I wish it were true now, you spoke of love as a woman with reserve. Think of a cello when you sing this music. Warm up your sound, make it vibrant and very legato:

"Marguerite's mood remains unchanged until you reach the poco più animato. This needs more color, a bit more fullness. She is saying 'When he goes away, it is always so terrible for me.' To emphasize this, I would make a portamento on 'son départ' and later stress 'ab-SEN-ce':

"When you sing 'Alors ma pauvre tête se dérange bientôt,' balance this phrase so that it prepares the public for the next phrase, 'Mon faible coeur s'arrête,' which rises to A-flat. Remember that a note such as this is not just a high note but the consequence of what has preceded it; it is the end of a thought, a line. Take time to breathe well when this phrase is completed. Let your sound die away before beginning 'Puis se glace aussitôt':

fai - ble coeur, S'ar - rê - te, puis_ se_ gla - ce

"Marguerite is being less general and more specific about Faust in the next section, so there should be more intimacy in your singing. Make the first two phrases light, like the words. She says, 'How I admire his walk and his gracious bearing.' Sing this as a confidence to the audience:

Sa mar - che que j'ad - mi - re, son

port si gra - - - ci - eux

"And in the next phrase, 'Sa bouche au doux sourire,' there must be a quality of almost blushing, as though you are nearly ashamed to be speaking out loud of 'his mouth' and 'his eyes':

Sa bouche au_____ doux_ sou - ri - re,

Then, when you sing of 'his voice,' this can be big; let the sound out:

Sa voix_____ en - chan - te - res - se

However, draw back with the two-note phrases of 'de sa main la caresse.' This must be very tender, very light; she is feeling 'the caress of his hand.' You must make the audience feel it as well with your voice:

de   sa   main,_de_ sa _ main _ la _ ca - res - - - se

Open up again on 'hélas,' and watch the three eighth notes on 'et son baiser.' They must be only touched with the voice, but still must have support and timbre:

D'une___   a - mou - reu - se   flam - me,

"You can give more with 'D'une amoureuse flamme,' for here she speaks of her feelings about herself, and consequently there is less reticence:

hé - las!_____   et   son   bai - ser,

"At the next change in attitude, più animato ed agitato, the notes must be very carefully thought out and prepared. Berlioz has placed rests in the vocal line to convey emotion; it is the same thing we found in Violetta's 'Ah! fors'è lui' and Gilda's 'Caro nome.' But you would not have a noble sound or produce the proper results if you attempted to observe each of these rests literally. So do not think of breathing; rather, give a breathless character to your singing. Let the audience feel rather than actually hear the rests by allowing the notes to continue to vibrate; they must not be clipped off.

"It is extremely important to observe well the two-note phrases that Berlioz puts in for contrast, such as those on 'fenêtre,' 'dehors,' and 'jour,' for example. They will help you immensely in shaping the line:

Je   suis   à   ma   fe - nê - tre,

"All of this agitato must build to 'O caresses de flamme!,' the most passionate moment in the scene. Here, and only here, Marguerite completely over-

comes the restraint she has felt earlier and is entirely open in her feelings for
Faust. This should be sung very full and with deep emotion. However, do not
stretch the line too much; you have to save breath for the low notes of 'flamme.'
If your line weakens towards the end of the phrase, you will have spoiled the
effect necessary here:

"This fullness should continue through to the final phrases, which must be
very measured. Take your time with 'dans ses baisers d'amour' and give it some
of the inner feeling with which you began the aria:

GOUNOD ❦ *FAUST*

ACT III: *Jewel Song*

"There is actually not much to do here. We have a young girl enjoying herself, taking pleasure in seeing herself transformed. You need to pronounce well, lean on the words, and have a good trill and even scales. Begin the trill right on the principal note; it is an expression of wonder, an exclamation. Sing the upward scale after the trill very legato, no chopping up of the notes, and go quickly, in strict rhythm. I would also make a decrescendo as you ascend, and touch the top G-sharp lightly:

Again, make the next A short but not hard; make it like a sigh. This is rapture, and sing with good legato on 'Est-ce toi, Marguerite' to contrast with the opening phrases:

Do not slacken the tempo with 'réponds, réponds, réponds vite'; there will be a temptation to do this because of the repeated words:

ré-ponds-moi, ré-ponds, ré-ponds, ré-ponds vi - te!

"Emphasize 'vi-SA-ge' and keep the music rolling with the scales on 'fille.' Also, I would crescendo as you go up these scales:

C'est la fil - - - le

"Do not slow up at 'C'est la fille d'un roi, qu'on salue au passage.' This should be in tempo. You can, however, broaden the music somewhat at 'S'il me voyait ainsi,' returning to tempo in the next phrase. Also, I would portamento from the G-sharp up to the B, then breathe:

S'il me vo - yait ain - si!___Comme u - ne de-moi-sel - le

A few bars later, 'Comme une demoiselle, il me trouverait belle' must also be exactly in tempo. On the repeat, however, you can use a little rubato and make your ritard on 'belle':

Comme u - ne de-moi-selle, Il me trou-ve - rait bel - le!

"The next section—'Achevons la métamorphose'—should be very clean, very even. The poco più lento must be stressed well; Marguerite is amazed at how different she looks covered with jewels. Give good color to 'Dieu' and 'main,' and little by little become faster so that when you reach the trill you are back to the original tempo. The repeat is like the beginning, and when you reach the coda, make it legato and big in sound:

ACT III:
Jewel Song

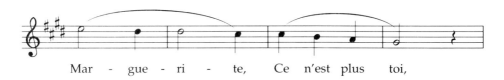

Mar - gue - ri - te,   Ce n'est plus   toi,

"Do not lose time with 'c'est la fille d'un roi.' This is in tempo. Breathe after 'salue' and try to sing through the high B in one breath. You can do it if you don't slow the tempo down on the trill. If you have to breathe, take a very quick one before the turn, and attack the B on 'ah':

Non!   c'est la   fil - le d'un   roi,_____   Qu'on sa -

- lue   au   pas - sa - - - (ah) - ge!

GOUNOD ❧ *ROMÉO ET JULIETTE*

ACT I: *"Je veux vivre"*

"Like Marguerite's Jewel Song, this aria for Juliette is simple and direct in feeling. She is at a party, happy, and everything around her seems like a dream.

"Begin the opening cadenza quickly, going straight to the high B-flat, which can be held. However, do not slow down after leaving the B-flat, and be very exact in your pitch—it is easy to lose your way here:

Ah!_____

"The aria should be light and always have a sense of motion. Watch carefully the acciaccature. Some are below the principal note and some are above; we must hear the difference. And make a good legato on 'vivre' and 'rêve' as a contrast to 'Je veux' and 'dans le':

The phrase 'm'enivre' up to A should open like a flower. Make a small ritard on the A, and bring the music back into tempo with 'Ce jour' which follows:

Do not overdo the phrase '. . . âme, comme un trésor' which goes up to A. It should be buoyant but more or less in tempo:

" 'Comme un trésor' returns again as a scale, and it must be exactly in tempo:

"Also, keep to the tempo with 'Cette ivresse de jeunesse' and make 'Ne dure hélas qu'un jour' very legato:

ACT I:
"Je veux vivre"

Cette i - vres - se de jeunes - - - se

ne dure hé - las____ qu'un jour,_____

The two phrases on 'Et le bonheur' must be contrasted—the first forte, the second piano:

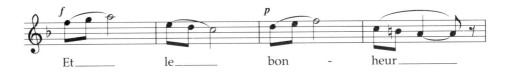

Et____ le____ bon - heur____

Make the chromatic scale on 'Ah!' as clean as possible and smooth—no accents!:

Ah_____ Je

"With the un poco meno allegro, take your time, abandon yourself to the music, be generous with your voice:

Un poco meno allegro, ma poco

Loin____ de l'hi - ver mo - ro - se,

"Again, the scales, when you return to tempo primo, must be like oil and must build to the trill on A. I would gradually make a crescendo on the four sets of downward scales from A. Take the time to breathe well before the trill, and be certain not to lose the gruppettino before the B-flat:

"Begin the final cadenza at once, and sing it very rapidly. Keep it moving straight through 'comme un trésor' without any slackening of the tempo:

"The final trills must be exact, and it is very important that we hear each of the turns that follow the trills; sing them on 'Ah!' For the conclusion, you may add a top C:

BIZET ☙ CARMEN

ACT III: *"Je dis que rien ne m'épouvante"*

"We have here a timid peasant girl, Micaela—the opposite of Carmen—and her music must be sung with simplicity and intimacy; it must come from deep within. Yes, she is frightened in this smugglers' lair, but her aria still must be very cantabile, flowing. Don't give too much voice. Even the fortissimo B in the middle section should not be held too long; it is terror, nothing else.

"In the recitatives, Micaela is talking to herself. Do not give it great importance; keep it moving, in fact, give the words urgency when she says, 'Il est ici, je le verrai' [He is here, I will see him]. Don José is the reason she has braved this terrible place; she wants to save him from Carmen:

"When you reach the E-flat on 'mère,' don't overdo it. In fact, it does not have to be held its full value. This is recitative, and the orchestra waits for you. The secret of recitative is giving and taking:

"Begin the aria itself very gently, very simply. Be certain to take a good breath before 'Mais j'ai beau faire'; you have a long way to go and will need it. Also, I would make a nice legato down from G to G, from 'j'ai' to 'beau':

ACT III:
*"Je dis que rien
ne m'épouvante"*

"Be careful not to lose the music's momentum when you reach the G of 'peur'; you will, if you hang on to this note. Keep the music moving, and in the next phrase be very careful of the turn; don't slow down for it, but we must hear each of the pitches:

"In the center section you can intensify the phrases, but this does not mean singing them loudly; this is not an aria for Carmen. Also, don't tighten up and push on the music in anticipation of the high notes. Let them come naturally as a consequence of her terror. Remember, she is scared, but says, 'I want to see this woman they tell me is so terrible':

"But when Micaela speaks of Carmen ('Elle est dangereuse, elle est belle'), it is said with goodness. This is the key to this tender creature:

"Begin warming up the phrases with 'Mais je ne veux pas avoir peur!' and keep the music moving towards the B. Breathe well before it and sing it exactly in tempo, then keep moving straight ahead. This ties the phrases together, and it's easier on you as well:

ACT III:
*"Je dis que rien
ne m'épouvante"*

"You can take time with the second 'protégerez,' but again the turn must be clean and precise. Breathe well before the high G, and place the sound well in your mind before singing it; it must be attacked in the middle of the note, then diminuendo and portamento to the lower G:

"When the first part of the aria returns, I would give it more color and emphasis than when you began. This is not entirely for contrast; the reason is more basic. In music, when you have the same phrase or phrases twice, one must be less important than the other, or else neither one will make an effect. Plan the return of this aria so that it forms a balance with the first part. As I said, I would give more the second time, especially on 'Seule en ce lieu sauvage':

"At the very end, you must be careful not to hold the fermata too long. It is not the real conclusion of the aria. If you give all your breath on the D, you will not be able to give full importance to the E-flat, which should have a crescendo and then a diminuendo:

MASSENET ❧ WERTHER

ACT III: *Air des lettres*

"Charlotte in *Werther* is a woman who has been suffering for a long while. She is married to a man she does not love but remains faithful to him despite the fact that Werther, whom she does love, loves her in return. She has saved Werther's letters, and in this scene she rereads them alone. While the piece is quiet and intimate, it must also be tense, because it prepares us for the tragedy to come—Werther's suicide. So along with the colors of nostalgia and memory there must also be a presentiment of disaster.

"This scene is very difficult, because you must never lose a feeling of intimacy yet you must convey terrific suffering. Bring this from deep within yourself. By your face (no smiles!) and your acting with your voice, you must make the public realize that Charlotte's life has become unbearable. You must think every moment what you are expressing; if you feel her anguish intensely, it will come out in your voice.

"Do not begin too softly. There must be great sentiment; Charlotte's whole soul is poured into one word at the beginning—'Werther.' Sing it the first time with feeling and with well-supported tone; even though this is French, notes must always be well placed and sustained. The second time, there can be more stress, more color. Though the markings here are only piano and mezzo-forte, remember that there must always be meaning, even when something is soft; the sound must come out. It will help if you lean on the *v* sound of 'Werther':

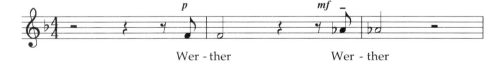

"In the next phrases, the aria itself, she is talking to herself, not to the audience. This does not mean that it should be whispered. When I say 'intimate,' I am speaking of an attitude, not of volume. You can sing out and achieve intimacy; it all depends on how you color a phrase. Start simply, and do not linger over notes; keep the music moving.

"One of the great differences between the French and the Italian school of singing lies in how one phrases. In Italian, individual words must be very clear, and certain key words are stressed to give a line shape. In French, however, the line moves more smoothly and without accents. For example, if this were Italian, you would sing 'qui m'aurait dit la PLA-ce,' making an accent at the top of the phrase. But in French all must be equal. We are concerned more with the entire phrase being equally balanced, never chopped up:

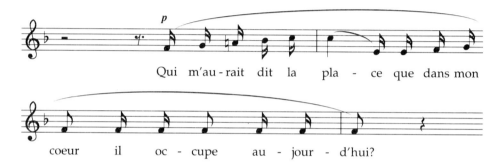

"In this first part of the scene, Charlotte is thinking, reading, brooding; but do not exaggerate—everything must be on an intimate scale. Yet do not overlook the sforzando on 'lasse,' and make a nice diminuendo after the accent:

"The first time you can begin to give is with 'Ces lettres!' This should not be prettily sung; there must be passion and great sadness in your voice. Also, make a good contrast between the first 'Ces lettres!' and the second:

"When you see 'Ah!,' as in the beginning of the next phrase, it does not necessarily mean you must breathe. In this case I would not—the phrase is better in one breath. But usually 'Ah!' is set apart from the balance of a phrase as an expression all its own. Yet—and this is what is difficult—it must always be a part of the whole:

Ah! je les re - lis sans ces - se

"Give good emphasis to 'Je devrais les détruire,' because Charlotte should destroy these letters but cannot bring herself to do so. Just afterwards, take your time on the eighth rest before 'je ne puis'; the orchestra will wait for you, and this phrase needs highlighting. But do it simply, with dignity:

Je de-vrais les de - trui - re je ne puis!

"Now we have a complete change in mood as she begins reading the letters. Werther tells her he writes from a small room; the weather is bad and he is alone. Your sound here should be eerie. You must sing his words with a chilly legato. Again, keep the music and the sound of your voice always ongoing, with all the notes weighted equally:

"Je vous é - cris___ de ma pe - ti - te cham - bre;

"At the end of this section, watch the three repeats of the word 'seul!' There must be contrast here; I would make the first simple, give the second more sound, and the last the least sound:

(lin) - ceul___ Et je suis seul!___ seul! tou-jours seul!"___

"Do not begin the next section too quickly. Here Charlotte looks up from her reading and again thinks aloud. Use the rests after the last 'seul' to look up and think. Then give the public her thoughts: 'Ah! no one is near him to give him tenderness or pity.' Do not give too much on 'Ah!' Here you will breathe after this exclamation, and then move the line along; don't drag the music, and don't sing too forte here. Remember the intimacy of her thoughts:

"Also, do not linger on 'Dieu!' Always remember that it is herself she is telling these things to. Move right through 'Dieu!' and straight on to 'et cet isolement?' This is the important thought. Sing it with deep feeling, connecting the notes carefully as you stretch the phrase for emphasis:

"Again, we have an abrupt change of mood. Now you can smile; Werther's letter recalls their happy times:

"When Charlotte answers his thoughts, add more intensity to your voice:

"The music is now building to a climax. Charlotte finally understands fully what she is involved in, the responsibility of this man's happiness and the fact that she has brought about the distressing situation between them. This must be very dramatic, almost terrifying. Keep your sounds more or less straight; do not vibrate too much or it will become melodramatic:

Ah! ce der-nier bil - let   me glace et m'é-pou - van - te!

"The next part is dramatic recitative. Do not overdo it, however. Stress the G-flat of 'crié,' but sing it in tempo. Then sing the D-flat to F of 'jamais!' quickly, and get on to the next phrase, 'On va bientôt'—the music must never lose its momentum:

"Tu m'as dit: à   No - ël,   et j'ai cri - é:_____

_____ ja-mais!   On va bien-tôt con - naî - tre

"Underplay the next G-flat. It is not what is important. The following phrase counts for more: 'Ne m'accuse pas, pleure-moi.' Here your voice should vibrate. When you repeat these words, make them very intimate, very sad. Be careful, however, not to overstay on the C of 'moi'—you have some very long phrases coming up for which you need a great deal of breath:

"Ne m'ac-cu - se   pas,_____   pleu - re - moi!"_____

"This final section must be intensely legato, but to obtain it you must leave each note sooner than written so that you can connect all together well. There is a real play of light and shadow here, and you must bring out this chiaroscuro. It is not a question of singing loudly or softly, but rather one of degrees of intensity. Feel the words deeply:

ACT III:
Air des lettres

"Oui,   de   ces   yeux   si   pleins   de   char - mes,

"Keep the remainder of the aria very simple and very alive. Again, do not oversing the last G-flat. What are more important are the final C's—'tu frémiras!' Weight them with sadness and with meaning:

tu fré - mi - ras!___   tu fré - mi - ras!

ACT III: *"Pourquoi me réveiller"*

"This aria is very straightforward and must be sung with feeling and simplicity. It is sad but also dreamlike. Never force it; no pressure on the voice, let it flow. Watch throughout for the single sixteenth notes. These must be precise so there is contrast with the eighth notes:

"Pour-quoi me ré - veil - ler,   ô souf - fle du prin - temps,_

"There is a climax to each of the two verses. When you come to the first, the F-sharp of 'temps,' don't close up. Keep the sound open and free. The same is true for the G-sharp that follows:

est   le   temps   Des   o - ra - ges

"Personally, I would be very sparing with the rallentando in the bar before the A-sharp, and go right to the high note. Don't waste time and don't hold it too long. You can hold it longer the second time, and there it will mean more. As the orchestra will wait for you here, take time for a good, full breath after the A-sharp so the next phrase can be taken in a single breath. Also, at the end of the long phrase the D-sharp and E-sharp must be clean; sing on the note. I would also make a portamento from E-sharp to F-sharp. Again, remember, there is a big difference between a portamento and a slide. In portamento we bring one note up to another and connect them; this is legato. A slide is scooping and is unmusical:

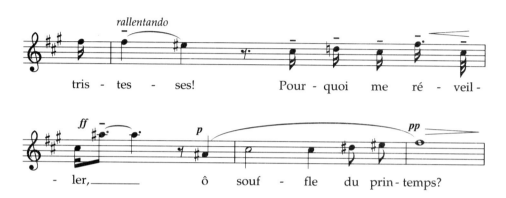

"The second verse continues like the first with a few important differences. Measure well the D's of 'ne trouveront plus,' attack well the F-sharp of 'Hélas,' and this time hold the A-sharp:

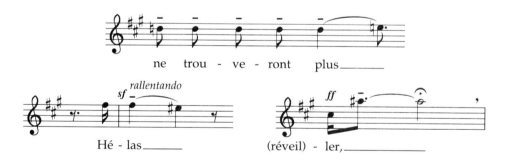

"Again, the final phrase is in one breath, but remember that you will need more air the second time, because the phrase ends forte instead of piano:

PONCHIELLI ✑ *LA GIOCONDA*

ACT II: *"Stella del marinar!"*

"This is a very nervous aria. Laura has been left alone in a strange place and is worried that her rendezvous with Enzo will be discovered. The entire piece is agitated; don't let down for a moment. It begins with a few lines of recitative. Move over them quickly, but take a little time on the D of 'Ah!,' though not too much on the D of 'Madonna.' Play down the accent there:

"The aria must be very impassioned. Accent well 'Santa' in 'Vergine SAN-ta':

Then make the next phrase very legato in contrast. Don't overlook the acciaccatura on 'ora,' and it is better not to breathe once you begin 'tu mi difendi' until after 'suprema':

"Also, take the phrase 'mi trasse a tale audacia estrema' in a single breath:

mi tras - se   a   ta - le au - da - cia e - stre - - - ma!

"When you reach the end of the first section, breathe well before attacking the E on 'Ah!' and then make a portamento down with great feeling to the C-sharp of 'scenda.' Take a quick catch breath after 'scenda' to get you through the remainder of the phrase:

e___ tre - ma.   Ah!   Scen - da per que - sta

"I wouldn't make too much of the stringendo at 'scenda sul capo mio,' because these notes need to be weighted well. Make it poco stringendo:

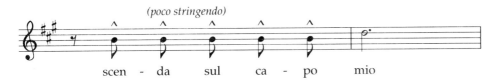

scen - da   sul   ca - po   mio

There is also room for a nice portamento on 'mio' from the C-sharp down to E:

sul ca - po   mi - o   u - na be - ne - di - zion___

As you come down from the F-sharp of 'discenda,' wait after the G-sharp to give the next phrase importance:

di - scen - da la tua be - ne - di - zio - ne,

"Be very rhythmic, even driven, with 'la tua benedizion.' Breathe after it, and don't hold the F too long, then finish the phrase. I would not sing the last notes on the words in the score. You'll get a better sound using these:

la　tua　be - ne - di - zion,　scen da su me,　su　me!

BOITO ✄ *MEFISTOFELE*

ACT III: *"L'altra notte"*

"In this aria, Margherita goes in and out of reality. It is a piece of contrasts, and you must have many different sounds—eerie, round colors—to bring it alive. Do not just vocalize here; the situation and the thoughts are not pretty. There must be a tragic, dramatic impact to your singing.

"Do not begin too slowly; let's have strong dynamics, a good legato, and a solid sound. Build the opening phrase upward to the F:

"Do not be afraid of letting your voice out on the low notes. You have got to use full chest voice here, and the sound on 'gittato' must be darkly covered:

"As I have pointed out several times, it has become a fad to say that if you sing chest notes you will have no high notes. This is not so. Listen to recordings of old singers who were well trained; you'll hear that they had both. This was the schooling. Besides, without good chest sounds, you cannot cut through an orchestra, nor can you convey so terrifying a thought as 'The other night, they threw my baby into the depths of the sea.'

"The next phrase must be exactly in tempo except at the very end, where

I would speed up a bit; a small accelerando on 'dicon ch'io' helps reinforce the sense of terror and pain that Margherita feels:

or per far - mi de - li - ra - re_di - con_ ch'io

"And keep the next phrase, 'l'abbia affogato,' still big. She is horrified that they say it was she who drowned the child. I would make the A at the end of 'affogato' a bit longer than written so that the phrase will not seem chopped off.

"Then the next phrase must be entirely different; her poor mind wanders off to another thought—'The prison cell is cold and dark':

l'ab-bia af-fo - ga - to.   L'au-ra è fred-da,   il__ car - cer   fo - sco,

Again, on 'e la mesta' you must use chest voice:

e   la me - sta   a - ni - ma mia

"The mood shifts again at 'come il passero del bosco vola.' She is delirious. In her mind, her poor soul is like a little bird flying, flying, flying. This is the reason behind the cadenzas here and at the end. They are not to show off your voice; they are to portray her sick mind. Don't drag these cadenzas out; keep them tight, quick. Also, divide each cadenza into four phrases, singing each phrase on 'vola':

co-me il pas - se - ro__ del__ bo - sco   vo - la,

vo - la, vo - la, vo - la, vo - la via.

"Following the cadenza, you can change the words from 'pietà di me' to 'di me pietà,' whichever will give you the best low sounds on F to D:

Ah! pie - tà di me!
(di me pie - tà!)

"The second verse is almost the same as the first, except that I would give it a somewhat more tender feeling—more caress to the phrases. When you reach 'e la mesta,' carry the phrase through the rests; ignore them, in other words. This will add urgency at this point, and by then it will be needed:

e la me - sta a - ni - ma mia

"Again, rephrase the final cadenza and ending as you did the first:

vo - la,_ vo - la, vo - la,

vo - la, vo - la via, ah!_di me_ pie - tà.

LEONCAVALLO ∽ *I PAGLIACCI*

PROLOGO

"Tonio the clown is introducing not only himself and his fellow players here but the opera as well. 'Don't be alarmed,' he says; 'the tears you will see are false, nothing is true.'

"It is of the utmost importance that your diction, your Italian, be beyond reproach, because so much of this Prologo is conversational and completely dependent on words; not until the end do you have a great melody to carry you along.

"Begin with authority, with importance—'Si PUÒ?' Let your voice out, relax, open your throat. There must be complete freedom to your singing, and though the first part is marked largamente, move it along so that the music does not drag:

"When the first lyrical section comes ('Poichè in iscena ancor'), double the cello line; you have a choice in the score of singing or speaking, but traditionally one sings the phrase:

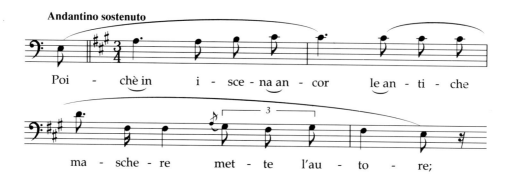

Sing this with the utmost elegance; you are offering the performance to the public. The next section ('Ma non per dirvi') is very conversational. It must have a spring to it, a bounce like the cello line that accompanies the voice, yet there must still be authority:

Be careful not to overdo this; Tonio is reassuring the public that this is only theater, not real life, so it must be drama, not melodrama. Watch the word 'lacrime.' It is 'LA-cri-me,' not 'La-CRI-me':

"At the meno mosso, don't let the momentum of the piece drop. He is saying 'The author has tried to draw a bit of life,' and you must sing these phrases in that mood. In other words, they must be natural, almost like speech. Throughout this part, be very careful of your vowels; they carry the line. Point this recitative to the E-flat of 'uom.' You can hold this note, for Leoncavallo gives you a tenuto here. It is the climax of the section and the thought is important: 'It is his [the author's] principle that the artist is only a man':

"Again the mood shifts. The next part must be really legato; sing it as if you were a cello, but remember, even though it is piano, it must be well supported:

In the middle of this section, some scores have an alternate E on 'singhiozzi,' but I would sing the C as written:

There may be a tendency to slow down at 'il tempo gli battevano!' before the tenuto; the line, however, must drive to the tenuto or it will not have meaning:

"In the animando, there must be a good, full sound on the low C's; here, you can lean hard on your consonants to help bring out these low notes:

In the next phrase it should be 've-DRE-te de l'O-dio i TRI-sti frut-ti':

And at 'urli di rabbia, udrete, e risa ciniche!' your singing must be like a hammer pounding out the notes; you are driving to the climax of the aria. Take a good, deep breath before 'e risa' so that you can make a crescendissimo on the E-flat of 'ciniche':

"Now you are ready really to *cantare*. Give us big, generous phrases in the andante cantabile; put your whole soul into it:

On the E-flats of 'considerate,' you must phrase up and into the F that follows. I know this portamento is not written, but here it is needed. These are things that must be done to give an important passage its full due:

"It is also traditional—and good, I think—to add an A-flat at the end of this section; it brings the line to a full conclusion it would otherwise lack. There are two ways to leave this high note, depending on which is the more comfortable for your voice. You can either portamento from the A-flat to the F on 'voi' or breathe after the A-flat and begin the next phrase on F, continuing the line down to D-flat, B-flat, E-flat, D-flat:

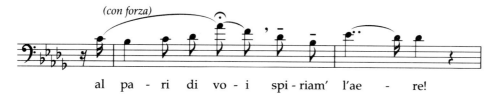

or

"The final part, più lento, is nearly spoken; in fact, it is recited on the notes. Keep it simple:

PROLOGO

"Deliver 'Andiam' with full authority, and a high G can be added at the very end. Go straight to it; I would sing 'in-co-min-' all on eighth notes. Do not leave the G by a glissando or slide. This is in very bad taste. It is done frequently, but it is wrong. It can be legato—but *glissato,* never!:

ACT I: *Ballatella*

"As you begin this aria, remember that Nedda is terrified by a look she has just seen in the eyes of her husband, Canio. 'How burning was that look!' she begins. Give this opening its full meaning; put Nedda's fears on your face as well as in your voice. Your diction must be very clear here, yet you must convey a feeling of being nervous, lost, not quite aware of your surroundings:

I have heard this aria sung in much too cute a manner; in fact, there is a tendency for sopranos to sing anything marked piano in a cute way. This is wrong. There must always be dignity to whatever you do onstage, even if it is a comedy role or the part of a humble girl like Nedda.

"This aria has many different moods typical of Nedda. She is a carefree woman who wants her lover, enjoys her youth, and is full of passion. She has her fears but quickly turns away from them, saying 'Basta'—'Enough; it's just a bad dream.' The first change comes after the tense opening. 'Oh,' she says, 'what if he caught me, brutal as he is?' She is afraid Canio will learn she loves someone else. You do not have to exteriorize, however, to convey this idea to the public. Underplay it, in fact; bring it from inside you on the phrase 'Oh, s'ei mi sorprendesse.' Make the B-flat or 'Oh!' short, clean, and on pitch. Do not use too much breath here; breathe, and then move right up to the G forte. This will be expressive enough:

Give strong meaning to 'brutale': let's hear the *r*:

"Now the mood shifts once again. She can't be bothered to think of Canio anymore. From here to the end the atmosphere is carefree. Sing 'Ma basti' in an easy way; in other words, throw it away. Emphasize, however, 'son questi' in the next phrase:

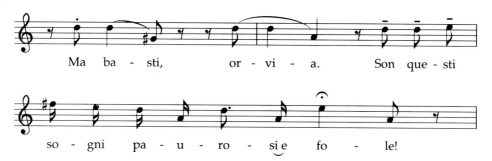

"Attack the A in the next section gently, lovingly, but do not hold it longer than written. Sing right through the line, slackening your pace only at 'mezz'agosto,' and then only a little:

Emphasize 'PIE-na di vita'—'I am *full* of life':

Give special meaning as well to 'arcano desìo,' this 'mysterious desire' which grips Nedda:

"The next section must be animato, but very simple. The birds overhead remind Nedda of her past, of her mother. If you give too much emphasis and voice here, what will you do later when the aria must build to its finish?:

"Attack the trills before the aria right on. Do not begin slowly and build; there isn't time. These trills must be fast and brilliant:

"Keep the aria itself simple and direct. At the beginning what it needs is good, clean singing:

"The first change comes with 'lasciateli vagar'—'let them roam, these free birds.' Slightly slacken the pace here; make this phrase bigger than the others. Nedda is thinking of herself, her freedom:

"The animando, 'Che incalzi il vento,' must be very rhythmic and press forward:

Accent well 'e vanno, e vanno,' and later make the G-sharp of 'mar' big:

"When the first part of the aria returns—'Vanno laggiù'—make it bigger; remember we are driving to the finish at this point:

" 'E van' appears four times at the end. Each one must be bigger, until the last is the biggest of all. You will need a good breath before this last note so that you can really crescendo on it to bring the aria to a full conclusion. Make certain you cut off this note exactly with the orchestra:

ACT I: *"Vesti la giubba"*

"Unlike most recitatives, this one before Canio's famous aria 'Vesti la giubba' must have great emphasis, great importance. Make each word count, but without overdoing it. Let's have no sobbing here. It is rare that one can get away with such exaggerations. Gigli did, but I must say I disliked it; he cried too much in his singing. You can convey the heartbreak of Canio being betrayed without sobs. There must be nobility to this aria as well:

And it is 'DI-co,' 'FAC-cio,' and 'D'UO-po':

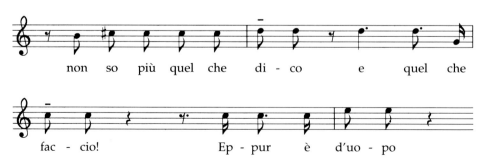

From 'Eppur è d'uopo,' keep the recitative moving straight up to the high A. Again, do not overdo the laughter; measure it carefully. You can take time with the phrase 'Tu se' Pagliaccio!' It is the end of the recitative and sums up Canio's feelings:

"The aria itself must be very straightforward, almost declaimed. Diction is of the utmost importance here. You must always listen to what you are saying and be fully aware of the words. One of the bad habits even good singers can fall into is delivering words automatically. Sometimes, they are incorrect or accented wrong, and we simply do not hear the mistake. I always had someone at a rehearsal with paper and pencil listening to me, writing down mistakes I had fallen into and no longer heard. A singer's concern for line and for a good sound often leads to bad diction.

"Incidentally, in this opening phrase you can portamento on 'infa-,' but again don't overdo it:

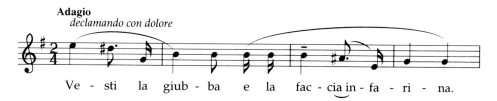

We need a good accent on 'paga' and then carry the E of 'qua' up to the G and breathe before beginning 'E se Arlecchin':

Get the low D's of 'applaudirà' as firm and full as possible. I know these notes are difficult in the tenor voice, but they will sound if you accent well and trust your consonants. You can, however, if you wish, sing the alternate F-sharps:

ACT I:
"Vesti la giubba"

ap - plau - di - rà!

"Take a deep breath before the F-sharp 'Ah!' You'll need it, for the next phrase must be, if at all possible, in a single breath:

e il do - lor   Ah!____   Ri - di, Pa - gliac - cio,

Do not hold the first A too long, for this phrase as well should be in one breath:

sul   tuo   a - mo - re in fran - to!

Save your greatest expression not for the A's but for the descending line 'Ridi del duol che t'avvelena il cor.' Breathe well before 'il cor'; really take your time here for emphasis, and give each word ('il cor') great accents without being vulgar. Above all, do not slide into these notes. They must be attacked well and must be on pitch. Find a good way to sing both the notes and express Canio's heartbreak, and then stick to it. Don't do something different each time:

Ri - di del duol che t'av - ve - le - na il   cor!____

MASCAGNI &⁓ *CAVALLERIA RUSTICANA*

"Tu qui, Santuzza?"

"You have to know how to sing and be sure of yourself to sustain this piece. Santuzza and Turiddu are a pair of hot-blooded Sicilians who are at each other's throats. But you must make their passions clear while maintaining the proper rhythms and pitches of this duet, without exaggeration.

"Turiddu begins angrily. He is upset to see Santuzza; he knows he has misused her, that he is in the wrong. This makes him uneasy. This opening dialogue must be in sharp, etched rhythm, but with a well-supported sound. Accent 'San-TUZ-za':

"Turiddu should make his second line, 'È Pasqua, in chiesa non vai?' a little less abrupt; give a bit more, with irony. He knows why she is not going to church. And Santuzza's answer should be hard—'NON VO':

"Tu qui, Santuzza?"

"Santuzza must make a contrast between the two phrases 'Debbo parlarti'; I would make the second more accented, more insistent. Turiddu should answer quickly with 'Qui no!' Watch carefully your pitches here—G-flat to D-flat, G-flat to F-flat:

"As this section continues, there must be the feeling that each continually interrupts the other. Keep the phrases moving. With Santuzza, it is withheld fury; with Turiddu, it is impatience. Turiddu can be a bit softer at 'Santuzza, credimi'; he is trying to calm her. But she will have none of it, and lashes back with 'No, non mentire' [No, don't lie]:

"In the andante section which follows, Santuzza begins with her emotions more under control, but suddenly they burst out again at the end of the phrase 'scorto presso l'uscio di Lola':

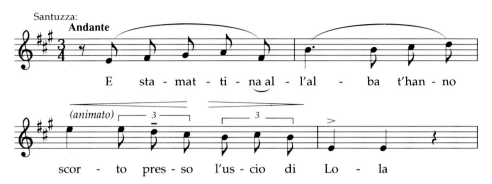

"Turiddu's voice must strike out at her with 'Ah! mi hai spiato!' [Ah! you were spying on me!]. Santuzza must in turn sing the E of 'No!' almost violently to keep the tension going:

Then, however, she quickly softens her approach; she is afraid of going too far, of irritating him too much:

"Don't let go of the line beginning 'Oh! questo non lo dire.' This is almost fright; get over it quickly:

"After 'lasciami dunque,' Turiddu must really be strong and angry. Sing his words here with great force. I would breathe right before 'colla tua pietà,' so that you can accent well 'COL-la':

"At 'L'ami, l'ami,' Santuzza must really warm up her voice and the phrases; she is desperate:

And at 'Quella cattiva femmina,' she is furious as well:

"With the con forza, Turiddu must be careful not to drag. I would breathe after 'Santuzza' and give a good accent to 'schiavo':

"When Santuzza replies, it must be very legato, very full. Breathe after 'insultami' and 'perdono':

At the conclusion of this long phrase, accent well the final 'l'angoscia mia':

"Keep this whole section tight; it mustn't sag. At the end, decide together where you wish to breathe. I would take the breath just before the C to the upper A:

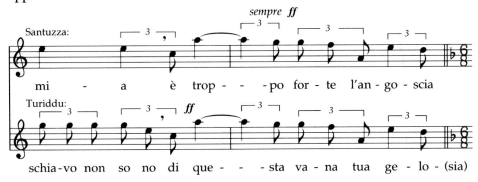

"After the interruption of Lola, Turiddu picks up the duet with even greater anger:

"Santuzza responds to him coldly. Following 'e ben ti sta,' Turiddu must take time to strongly accent 'Ah! per Dio!'; he has finally lost all patience with Santuzza:

"Tu qui, Santuzza?"

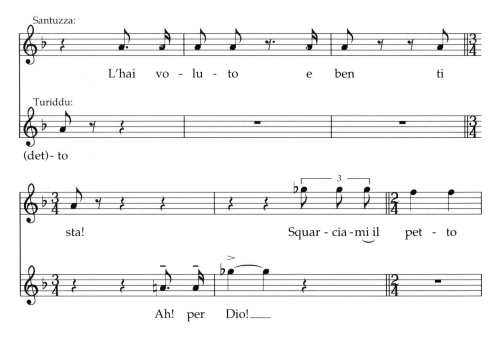

"Before the big A-flat section, the phrase 'Turiddu, ascolta!' must be sung very passionately; Santuzza is desperate to get him back:

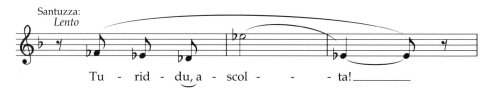

"Santuzza must be generous in the next section; really give your voice. Feel the music deep within yourself rather than thinking of the notes. Begin with a good *o* sound; I would carry the E-flat of 'No' up into the F that follows. But remember: *portato,* not *glissato.* I would also breathe after the first 'rimani'; it will point up the repetition of the word—she is begging him to remain, to listen to her:

"And when she says 'dunque tu vuoi abbandonarmi' you must use your chest voice for the end of the phrase to the low C:

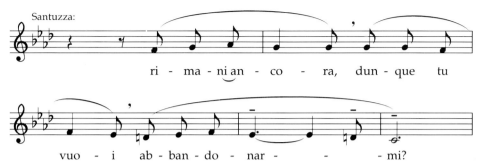

ri - ma - ni an - co - ra, dun - que tu vuo - i ab - ban - do - nar - - mi?

"When the passage 'No, no, Turiddu' returns it must be even more generously sung. Give the public Santuzza's southern soul. Once again, carefully plan your breathing when singing with another person. There are subtle ways in which one singer can remind the other of a breath during performance —a look in the eye, a press of the hand. In this section, I would breathe before the second D. Santuzza will have to make a slight adjustment in her vocal line, however, so that she will not be taking her breath in the middle of 'rimani':

no, Tu - rid - du, Tu-rid - du ri - ma - ni an - co - - ra.

Per - chè se - guir-mi, per - chè spi - ar - - mi?

"After the four bars of orchestral music, Santuzza must bring great sadness to 'La tua Santuzza,' but without dragging the music. Keep it rhythmic:

La tu a San - tuz - - za

Diminuendo on 't'implora,' then breathe and attack 'come cacciarla' forte:

pian-ge e t'im-plo - - ra _____ co - me cac - ciar - la

"At the time change, the music must move. When Santuzza and Turiddu begin shouting at one another—'Va!' 'No!' 'Va!'—make certain these notes are exactly on pitch and held their full value. This happens a second time after the big grandioso section, and you must be even more careful to watch your pitches, because there is less time than before:

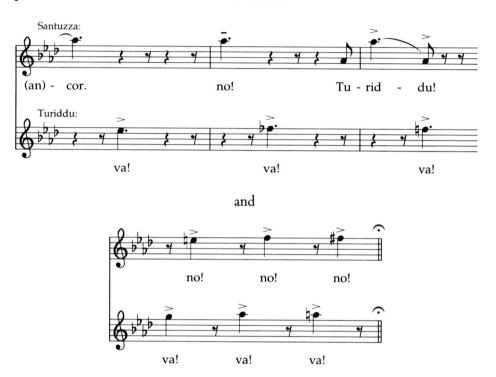

and

"At the andante molto sostenuto, Santuzza must plead with great expression; she is almost crying here. This is one of those places where you must forget your voice and think only of the character and her misery. After 't'implora,' you will sometimes hear a singer scoop up to the F. This is bad taste, even though she is begging. Besides, you should breathe deeply after 't'implora' and make a fresh, good attack on the F of 'CO-me'—*'How* could you drive your Santuzza away?':

When she repeats this, it must be even bigger:

"Tu qui, Santuzza?"

When the time changes to 6/8, don't slow down; keep the music moving:

"Let the orchestra finish its measure of fortissimo and ritardando before taking the top B-flat. This note must be carefully measured; I would suggest two beats. Both singers, however, must agree on this. The conductor will wait for you; he has no choice. It is your responsibility not to overdo the note. Attack it, breathe well, and come down quickly:

"It is more effective to eliminate the 'ah!' before the maestoso; it will also give you the chance for a really good breath, which you will need in this last section:

"Tu qui, Santuzza?"

"As you go up to the A-flat, I would change the words in Santuzza's part; it is easier to ascend on 'ancora,' I think, than on 'Turiddu.' The last note should be very short:

"There is only tremolo in the orchestra at the 2/4, so take your time. These insults at the end must not be rushed. Turiddu's 'Dell'ira tua' may be spoken rather than sung:

"At the very end, Santuzza also has a choice open to her with 'A te la mala Pasqua.' It can be either spoken forcefully or sung on the pitches in a quasi-parlato way. I prefer the latter. It is harder but more effective. It needs,

however, furious accents. Just to sing it is not enough. Afterwards, breathe   *"Tu qui, Santuzza?"*
well, wait and hammer out 'spergiuro,' with a good portamento down to the
lower A-flat:

A   te   la ma-la   Pa-squa,   sper - giu - ro!

PUCCINI ✤ *MANON LESCAUT*

ACT III: *"Guardate, pazzo son"*

"This is a desperate moment in the opera, and it must be as dramatic as possible, but without exaggeration. Puccini has given you everything necessary to create great passion. You need only give in return the hot Italian blood of this piece. Remember, Des Grieux is almost mad at the thought of losing Manon. He tells the captain of the ship on which she is being deported that he will do anything —even scrub the deck—to accompany Manon. We must have every word; you must feel every word.

"In the first line, 'Ah! guai a chi la tocca!' I would leave out the eighth rest after 'Ah!' Otherwise this exclamation is cut too short and is less heated. Accent it well:

"Make 'Ah! non v'avvicinate!' just as strong, and hammer out evenly each quarter and eighth note of 'Chè, vivo me, costei nessun strappar potrà!' When you reach the upper A, hold it and then ride it down to the lower one. I am always for what is written in a score, but there are certain moments, and this is one, when you have to do a bit more than is asked for. This high note needs more importance than it is given in the score; it is the climax of this fierce recitative:

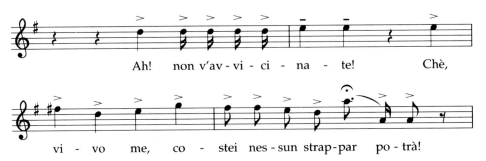

"Just before the aria begins, sing the first 'No!' forcefully, the second a little less so and with more heart, and then emphasize well 'pazzo son,' breathing deeply before beginning 'Guardate':

"Though the aria itself is marked largo sostenuto, it must always be kept moving; never let it drag. And even where it is marked ritardando or allargando, it should be more a question of weighting or accenting the phrase rather than slowing it down. I would, however, hold the F-sharp of 'chiedo,' because it marks the close of the aria's first section:

But do not slow down for the sixteenth notes of 'ed io verrò,' or later the rising line of 'Ah! guardate, io piango.' Also, in this latter phrase, breathe after 'guardate' but not after 'piango':

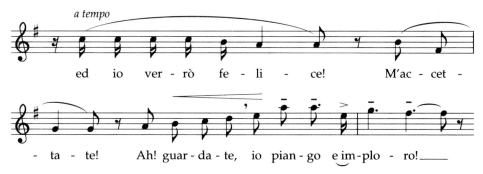

"Watch your words at 'Vi pigliate il mio sangue'; we must have them all. And it is 'la VI-ta,' with no breath afterwards:

"On the climactic phrase of the aria, the high B, there are three different ways this may be phrased. As each voice is different, there cannot be a single rule for where to breathe. Try them out and see what suits your voice. First, you can breathe before the B:

Or you can breathe after the B:

Or, perhaps best of all, breathe before the first and after the second of the two 'pietà's on either side of the B:

However you breathe, make certain it is a full breath, one that will carry you through this difficult section.

ACT IV: *"Sola, perduta, abbandonata"*

"This aria is an expression of great sadness and great fear. But be careful not to oversing it; you'll kill yourself. Remember, you have a long way to go. Clean pronunciation and a good sense of the words will see you through:

Give special emphasis to 'Orror! intorno a me':

At 's'oscura il ciel' Puccini asks you to *portare la voce,* but do it quickly, at the last moment and in rhythm. Don't drag it out, and above all don't glissando. And I would sing the phrase just afterwards, 'Ahimè, son sola!,' in chest:

You will need your chest voice again for 'io la deserta donna':

"Do not overdo the B-flat the first time; it comes again, and there must be a contrast between the two:

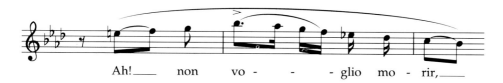

" 'Terra di pace' must be sung lightly:

When both phrases are finished, breathe well and wait before beginning the allegro vivo.

"This allegro must be sung with great abandonment; she is delirious. This section has to be built carefully, so that Manon's A at the largo molto sostenuto is the logical consequence of the ranting that precedes it:

and later:

I know Puccini instructs that 'tutto è finito' be parlato, but it is in better taste to sing these words on pitch. Color them with great emotion, and take a good breath just before.

"After 'ora la tomba invoco' the next phrases—'no, non voglio morir'—are like dramatic recitativo. Do not rush through them. It should be 'No [*breath*], non VO-glio mo-rir [*wait*], NON VO-GLIO MO-RIR!' And this time, hold the B-flat, but with good taste—don't overdo it:

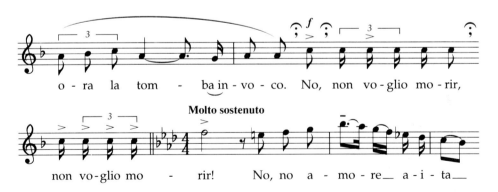

PUCCINI ✑ *LA BOHÈME*

ACT I: *"Che gelida manina"*

"Don't give undue importance to this aria either in voice or in tempo. It is simple; Rodolfo and Mimì are simple people. What you must give importance to is the words. He is telling her precious lies, flirting with this girl he likes —but lightly, not seriously.

"Start piano, sweetly and well supported. Watch the A-flat of 'cercar.' Make a good attack in the middle of the note, and don't slur down to the F:

Throughout this first section and 'Ma per fortuna è una notte di luna,' be very calm. Persuade Mimì gently. You want her to relax and forget the key she has lost but which you have found and hidden. Be careful of the turn on 'notte'; don't expend too much time or breath on it or the line will sag:

Make certain the E-flats of 'luna' are neat and clean in pitch. You can give more in the next phrase as Rodolfo becomes more insistent:

"Another spot where you must resist scooping is 'le dirò con due parole.' The A-flat of 'chi son' must be sung in the middle of the note:

(A) - spet - ti si - gno - ri - na, le di - rò con due pa - ro - le chi son, chi

"Don't overdo the high B-flat, and use the breath Puccini gives you after 'faccio' for expression, to emphasize 'come vivo,' which follows:

son,   e che fac - cio, co - me__ vi - vo.

"At the andante sostenuto—'Chi son? chi son? Sono un poeta'—keep the music moving; don't slow down:

son?__   chi son?   So - no un po - e - ta.

Put 'Scrivo. E come vivo? Vivo,' on your face as well as in your voice.

"In the next section, andante lento, he is very simple again. Don't over-extend yourself in this section; it is a chance to relax and prepare for the big phrases coming up. If you tire yourself before 'Talor dal mio forziere,' it will not be as generous in sound as it must be.

"This entire sostenendo largamente must be full and ardent. It leads the audience and prepares it for the climax of the aria—the high C of 'la speranza!' Remember, a C is not always the same. The note depends on what precedes it. You can have a good C in one aria and a less good one in the next. So we have to figure out each one each time.

"For this one, take a deep, full breath after 'stanza' and go right up. If you drag it out too much and do not prepare it, you will not have all the support you need:

stan - za   la_____ spe - ran - za!_____

" 'Or che mi conoscete' is quiet, but he is insistent once again with 'Deh! parlate, chi siete?' The aria then ends pianissimo as Rodolfo again asks Mimì to tell him who she is.

ACT I: *"Sì, mi chiamano Mimì"*

"Mimì is an adorable, plain girl. I don't know if the real Mimì was like this, but Puccini makes her this way. In this aria she is telling a story, so, as in Rodolfo's aria, the words are extremely important. Be very aware, too, of your face. Before you sing a note, you must give the emotion to the public on your face.

"Never practice, however, in front of a mirror. Mirrors are for dancers. Inside of you is the mirror you must use, a mental mirror. Never forget that a look—a frown, a smile—is an expression that must support the music. Use only the expression that is proper for what you are singing, for your face will tell the public as much as the music. Be particularly careful on nights when you are not at your best. Don't frown if something goes wrong. This is something I had to fight. It is one of the many bad habits you can get into unless you are careful and think to change it.

"Also, along with the notes of an aria and your facial expressions, you must carefully plan the situation. Who is this girl? What is she feeling? What is she all about?

"Watch your hands as well; don't move them too much. In fact, the less you move them, the better. If you constantly point here or there, the public will not believe you when it counts. Remember, there must always be a reason when you use your hands. When I began my career, the old style prevailed —big, grand gestures like those in silent movies. I had to fight this; I knew they were wrong. Everything today is more real, and the public expects realism from you on stage. Why should opera be different?

"Begin the aria with a smile, not only because it is appropriate to Mimì at this moment but because the more you can smile, the cleaner your diction will be, and the more receptive the public will be. The first note—'Sì'—must be a good tone and held for its full value. Don't let the beginning drag or become too heavy. Keep it simple, light, and only slightly accented: 'Mi chiamano Mi-MÌ.' Breathe after 'Mimì,' and be careful not to slight the sixteenth note of 'mio.' Sing it in rhythm, and I would portamento from G-sharp to the E of 'nome è.' Also, keep the vowels moving, and place your consonants within the stream of vowels:

ACT I:
"Sì, mi chiamano
Mimì"

"Let's have good, full low notes on 'ricamo in casa e fuori,' and do not change the tempo here. Secure low notes are just as important as secure high ones. This is all part of bel canto, which is the only way to sing. Lilli Lehmann, Malibran, Pasta all had their chest notes. You must too.

"In the next phrase, don't lose 'e' in 'Son tranquilla e lieta,' and give less sound to 'ed è mio svago far gigli e rose':

"The andante calmo must be caressed as much as you can. Make it very legato, but don't slow the music down or cheat on the rhythm. Also, a conductor can wait only so much for you here; you must work your expression within the possibilities of the orchestra:

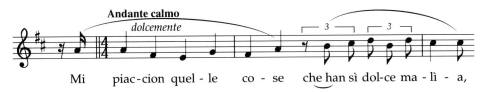

You should still be smiling with your voice and your face at 'che parlano d'amor,' and give more sound on 'di primavere.' Be careful of the second G-sharp of 'primavere.' Sing it in tempo; don't hold on to it:

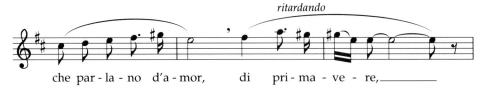

Keep the next phrases rolling, and do not linger too long on the fermata of 'cose.' You must take a good breath after 'che han nome' to set off 'poesia.' This is what the aria is about; it is the key to Mimì—she is poetry:

"When the first phrase of the aria returns, sing 'il perchè non so' exactly in time. The staccato marks do not mean to rush:

"The allegretto moderato is another example of a spot where you must fit your expression within the maestro's tempo. The orchestra cannot wait for you here. Keep this section very legato, and don't lose the turn on 'vado':

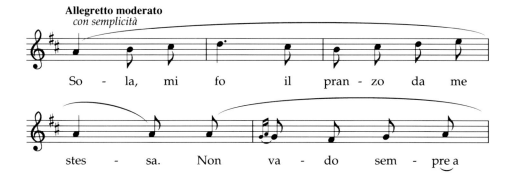

Though Puccini says 'a piacere' at 'Vivo sola, soletta,' make it legato, not staccato—no coyness!:

"At the poco rallentando, build the A of 'cielo'—and remember, only one *l*—up into a B to anticipate the next phrase, but add the B only at the last moment. Then breathe deeply, giving your breath as an expression of rapture to the public, before beginning 'Ma quando vien lo sgelo.' This portamento to B is not written, but it can be a lovely effect if well done—if not, forget it:

"Aim 'Ma quando vien lo sgelo' to the final word and lean on it: 'SGE-lo.' Breathe well, and give more voice for the next phrase, 'Il primo sole è mio.' This is the aria's one passionate moment: 'When the winter is over, the first sunshine is mine,' she sings, 'the first kiss of spring.' In 'Il primo bacio dell'aprile,' don't give too much on the first high A; save it more for the second:

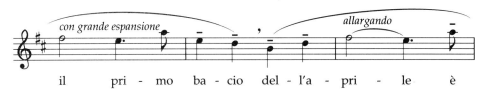

The second 'Il primo sole è mio' must be very generous, very legato, just as if it were Bellini. Puccini may be more modern, but he still must have his legato. Also, linger on the *mi-* of 'MI-o':

"Keep the final phrases very simple. 'My flowers,' she says, 'are not real': there is no sadness to this; it is just a fact. Watch well the portamento on 'faccio': don't overaccent it. The voice keeps on going from the E to the upper D. The '-cio' is simply added at the end; it is a consequence of the note before it. And just afterwards, give us all the *o*'s of 'hanno odore':

"The final recitative should not be strung out; keep it as natural as possible, with all the sixteenth notes exactly even. It must never be breathless; the words must be clean and clear. If you feel you are running out of breath in the second phrase—'sono la sua vicina che la vien fuori d'ora a importunare'—take a quick breath after 'vien,' but don't let the public know. 'FUO-ri' needs emphasis, as does 'im-POR-tu-na-re.' I would portamento from the F-sharp to the A of 'importunare' as well. And be certain your voice does not drop out on the final two D's. Vibrate the sound here so that the aria comes to a complete close:

ACT II: *"Quando me'n vo'"*

"Musetta is really an extravagant girl, yet with elegance, not vulgarity. She is very sure of herself and quite the opposite of Mimì, who would never dream of behaving as Musetta does in public. Musetta adores calling attention to herself; she has fun driving Marcello mad with jealousy.

"Begin her waltz in a good, flowing tempo. Above all, the aria must have allure—oomph. Your face must glow as you sing:

ACT II:
"Quando me'n vo'"

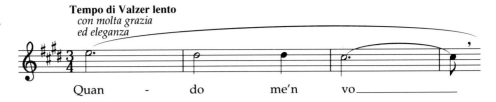

Do not, however, begin so full that you cannot give more voice at 'e la bellezza mia.' This phrase must be very generous; she is complimenting herself on her beauty. Just afterwards, do not hold the first B too long. There is time for that later. If you exaggerate the note here, the aria will lose its shape. What is important in this spot is the turn on 'me'; we must hear it cleanly. It is part of Musetta's sparkle. Also, the end of this phrase—'ricerca in me da capo a pie'—must be tossed off with humor:

"The next section should be sung directly to Marcello, so it can be more intimately scaled, but still insinuating:

"After this second section, which is continually in and out of time, you must be very strict with tempo at 'Così l'effluvio del desìo'; for this reason, keep the fermata of 'm'aggira' short, and do not be too espansivo with 'felice mi fa.' It should have rapture but not drag; this is more a question of attitude than of tempo:

"When the waltz theme returns, sing it with *slancio,* throw it away. However, emphasize 'tu' in the second bar; with it, she is telling Marcello off:

"Really dig into him with the words 'So ben: le angoscie tue'; there is great irony here. Be certain to take full advantage of the acciaccatura on 'dir.' It is almost as if she were scratching his face with this note:

"When you come to the last high B, go straight up to the note. Hold it, but not to the point that you lose the spitefulness of 'senti morir!' Remember, too, that this aria is part of an ensemble which moves right on after your high note. The maestro will probably save his biggest fermata for the B in the ensemble a dozen pages later:

ACT III: *"Donde lieta uscì"*

"There is very little to do in this aria. It is all virtually the same mood, one of great sadness: Mimì is saying goodbye to Rodolfo. Keep it simple and deeply felt. As always with Mimì, words are of major importance:

Though you must hold back slightly at 'torna sola Mimì,' the next phrase— 'al solitario nido'—must not drag. Also, go right up to the A of 'ritorna'; sing the sixteenth note exactly in rhythm:

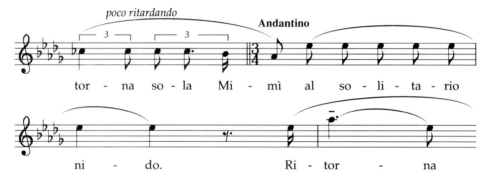

"Measure well the rests at the first 'Addio, senza rancor'; they will give the words importance:

"The next section must be very legato, just as you sang 'Mi piaccion quelle cose' in Mimì's first aria:

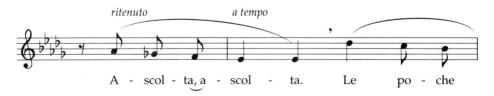

ro - be a - du - na che la - sciai spar - se.

Contrast well 'quel cerchietto d'or,' which should be very light, with 'e il libro di preghiere,' which must have more weight but is no louder:

quel cer - chiet - to d'or, e il li - bro di pre - ghie - re.

"Give more voice at 'Bada'; you must now lead the public to the conclusion of the aria. Notice that a few measures later Mimì says 'se vuoi' three times. Each must be different: loud, less loud, then a bit more. It is as if she starts to offer him the bonnet he gave her as a gift in Act II, then draws back, afraid that he won't take it, then resolves to offer it anyway:

Ba - da sot - to il guan - cia - le.____ c'è la cuf - fiet - ta

ro - sa. Se vuoi,____ se vuoi,____

se vuoi ser - - - bar - la a____ ri - cor - do

"In the last phrase, it is not 'senza' that is important but 'rancor.' Begin 'rancor' forte so that you can make a nice diminuendo on the note; if you begin mezzo-forte you will not have as effective an ending:

ad - dio, sen - za ran - cor.____

ACT IV: *"Vecchia zimarra"*

"This is a small piece, but it is of great importance; it is an aria people wait for. Sing it simply, in a charming, youthful way. This coat which you are now going to sell to help Mimì has been like a wife to you. It is so precious; it has warmed you, shared your experiences. To sell it is a great sacrifice. This is poetry in music, a small, beautiful jewel. Treat it as such.

"Begin very legato—emotion but not melodrama, no exaggerated darkening of your voice:

In the ninth measure, I would sing 'il' as a distinct sixteenth note and not as part of 'curvasti il,' as in the score:

Be careful of the E-flat of 'passar.' Sing right in the middle of the note; do not scoop up to it:

Later, be careful of your pitches at 'ti dico'; it is easy to go wrong here:

Take a big breath before and after the final 'addio's; they need great expression and importance. Don't throw this ending away. Vibrate your sound; make the words ring:

ACT IV: *"Sono andati?"*

"Here, I will deal only with Mimì's music. I would not begin this scene too softly. There should be power at the start, and moving expression. 'Are they gone?' she asks. 'I wanted so to be alone with you.' This needs vibrancy. Love the phrases here, but don't drag them:

There is a place for a tasteful portamento on 'Ho tante cose,' to emphasize the many things she wants to tell Rodolfo:

"A few measures later, I would also breathe after 'come il mare' to give importance to 'profonda,' which follows:

At 'Sei il mio amor,' really let your voice blossom out. Don't be afraid to give here; it needs passion, so open up. She is pouring out all her love for Rodolfo:

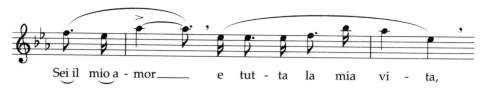

"The more delicate sections for Mimì come when she is remembering her first meeting with Rodolfo. The phrase 'Mi chiamano Mimì' must be quite different than in the first act. In Act IV it must sound tired, as if her strength is being drained from her. Yet always be precise in pitch—on the note. This is particularly true for 'il perchè non so':

"A page later, however, when Rodolfo gives her the bonnet she left behind, her strength seems to return. Here your voice must reflect Mimì's joy; it must not be cute. Fill the phrase with happiness:

"Watch at the allegretto, which follows, that you do not stretch the music too much and that all the eighth notes are sung with the same value:

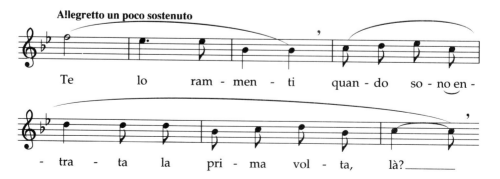

"Later, at 'E a cercarla' sing *Ed* a cercarla' if it helps you get the words out better. This section is like a gentle reproach to Rodolfo, a private joke between them. Play with the phrase when she says 'You said you were looking for the key, but I didn't believe you; I knew you had it all the time':

"I would sing 'lei la trovò assai presto' in one breath, making the turn on 'presto' clean and distinct:

This section and the reprise of 'Che gelida manina' as sung by Mimì must have a smile in the voice; these are lovely, dear memories she is recalling. Incidentally, it is 'Che gelida ma–NI–na':

" 'Oh come è bello e morbido' must not be too piano or too hesitant. Yes, she is dying, but it is a simple thing. Mimì's death is not a great tragic end, like Violetta's; rather, it is quiet and gentle. All the phrases at the end must be very legato. You can give a bit more at 'Tu! Spensierato!' Again, this is a sort of reproach—'How could you be so extravagant?' Then say 'grazie' lightly, and 'Ma costerà' [It costs a lot] with awe in your voice:

"When Rodolfo begins to cry, you must be like a mother or an elder sister comforting him. Her only concern as she dies is to make things easier for him, to console him:

Pian-gi?   Sto be - ne.   Pian-ger co - sì per - che?___

PUCCINI ❦ *TOSCA*

ACT I: *"Recondita armonia"*

"This aria for Cavaradossi is luxurious vocal material. He is painting a picture and steps back to look at it, speaking his thoughts out loud. He remarks that though he is painting a blonde, he loves a brunette—Tosca.

"The first two phrases of the aria are really like recitative, though not exactly. The thing is not to give them undue importance; they are only what is going on inside his head. Sing them very legato but very simply:

Re - con - di - ta ar - mo - ni - a   di bel - lez - ze di - (verse)

"Where you should open up is with 'E tu beltade ignota.' Warm up the phrases here, not only vocally but visually. Put a broad smile on your face; he's a happy man:

E   tu   bel - ta - de ig - no - ta___

"Again, we have a brief passage that is like recitative: 'L'arte nel suo mistero.' Keep it simple:

"Begin building for the end with 'nel ritrar costei,' but watch at 'Ah! il mio sol pensier sei tu' that you do not scoop to the high A and down from it:

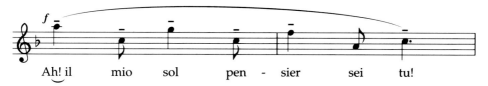

"Go straight to the B-flat and hold it. It's an easy note, so enjoy it. Save enough breath for the turn that follows, then breathe deeply and be generous with 'sei tu' to end the aria:

PUCCINI ✲ *MADAMA BUTTERFLY*

ACT II: *"Che tua madre"*

"Butterfly's music is treacherous, especially a section such as this which is so heavily weighted for the middle voice. You have to know how to sing very well to survive. An important consideration, then, is that this aria has movement and drive. Give it great feeling, which in turn will allow you to move it along and make it easier for your voice to sustain in the middle.

"Like Mimì, Butterfly is telling a story here, so we must have every word:

Also as in Mimì's arias, you must have good low notes here, especially 'la città'; the line must continue full down through the D-flat:

The next phrase I would break into two. Instead of 'a guadagnarti il pane e il vestimento,' sing 'a guadagnarti il pan' e il vestimento':

'La man tremante stenderà' must be very dramatic; bite into the words:

la man tre - man - te sten-de-ra!

"I would break the next phrases up into several smaller ones, because there should be a somewhat nervous, breathless quality to her words here; breathe after 'udite, udite,' after 'canzon,' and after 'carità':

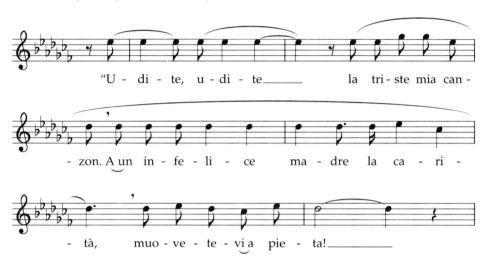

"U - di - te, u - di - te_____ la tri-ste mia can-

- zon. A un in-fe-li - ce ma-dre la ca-ri -

- tà, muo-ve - te - vi a pie - ta!_____

"The next section has an almost desperate quality to it; but it is a quiet desperation, just under the surface:

E But-ter - fly, or - ri - bi - le de-

- sti - no, dan - ze - rà per te!_____

Let your voice out at 'E come fece già,' and make 'La Ghesha canterà' very big:

E co-me fe-ce già_____ La Ghe-sha can - te-rà!

"We must have an immediate contrast for 'E la canzon giuliva e lieta in un singhiozzo finirà.' Begin very gently, almost sadly, then breathe after 'lieta,' and begin to build your voice again, making a crescendo on the F-sharp at the end:

"Now, you must really drive your voice and the music. Breathe after 'Ah! no!' and 'no! questo mai!':

I would make a portamento from the E-flat to the G-flat of 'porta,' then attack the A-flat and the high B-flat right on the note and come down cleanly each time—no slurs:

There must be a big crescendo on the last note of 'Mai più danzar!' Be careful how you begin the G-flat. If you give too much tone at the outset, there will not be enough for the crescendo. Measure this carefully:

The two A-flats in the next phrase are difficult to sing exactly in time and on pitch, but you must. Don't slight them:

The final A-flat must also be attacked dead center, and 'morta' sung harshly but on the pitches written. Make the first syllable the biggest—'MOR-ta!':

GIORDANO ❧ *ANDREA CHÉNIER*

ACT III: *"Nemico della patria"*

"The beginning of this aria is actually all recitative. Gérard is reading the indictment he has just signed against Chénier and reflecting on its words. This section must be very rhythmic and your diction as clean and forceful as possible. The high point of this first section is the outcry 'Traditore!' Build towards it.

"The aria itself begins with 'Un dì m'era di gioia.' This must be very legato and sustained at the beginning. Where you must open up is with 'Gigante, mi credea! Son sempre un servo!'—'I thought I was a giant, but I am still a servant. I only changed masters.' This must have great irony and contrast to it:

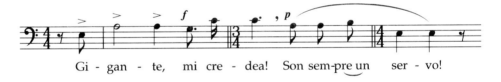

"Then, when he says 'I kill and tremble, and when I kill I cry,' you must give these words with great feeling. They are terrible words of dark sentiments. Be careful, however, that you sing the pitches exactly, especially on 'Ah! peggio,' which is often, and incorrectly, spoken instead of sung:

"The next section is again like recitative and leads to a big lyric moment which must be free yet affrettando:

La co-scien - za nei cuor ri - de - star__ de le gen - ti!

"Take a good breath before the F-sharp of 'bacio'—not only is the word important, but the note is the climax of the aria. Love the note—open your throat and the phrase will come easier. This sort of rich phrase is typical of the generosity of this composer, and you must repay his generosity. This is a place where you have to let yourself go. We may do our study at home, but eventually we have to forget work and simply sing, as here.

"At the very end, weigh carefully 'tutte le genti amar!,' but save breath to build the final note so that the aria will come to a complete and exciting conclusion:

tut - te le gen - ti a - mar!

CILÈA ✌ *ADRIANA LECOUVREUR*

ACT I: *"Io son l'umile ancella"*

"This aria must be sung very simply. 'I serve genius,' Adriana says. 'The author gave me the possibility to serve with his words, and I in turn give them from the heart.' You must take care not to overdo this piece; there is a tendency with this aria to give too much.

"Begin 'Ecco, respiro appena' with a good, clear sound. It should be tender and soft, but not childish. Prepare the phrase well in advance. Never, with any piece, just open your mouth at the last minute. Also, stop, think, and feel the pause deeply just before the aria begins:

"Begin the aria like a violin, staying close to the arch of the line. Make certain your sound is well supported; it mustn't drop even at piano. I would breathe after 'ancella,' 'creator,' and 'favella':

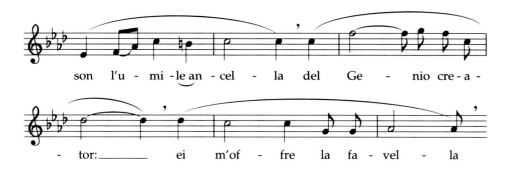

"In the second section, bring out the word 'dramma,' and use your chest voice, though without exaggeration, at 'vassallo della man':

"In the final third of the aria, budget your breath well so that you can make a good crescendo on 'gioconda.' And no portamento from the C to the A-flat in the next phrase!:

"The final phrase must be, as Cilèa asks, with a thread of voice, yet it must not be too piano or there will be no support for the line. And it is important that the portamento octaves in the next-to-last measure be sung as rhythmically accurately as possible and not with glissandi. Don't hold the high G too long. The impact should come with the A-flat. Breathe well before this last note so that you can give the public a good crescendo and then a diminuendo at the end:

ACT II: *"Acerba voluttà"*

"For this aria, you must lean especially hard on the words so that you will get past the orchestra, which is playing heavy fortissimo chords. But remember, when you have to fight to be heard, pronunciation is your best weapon.

"Do not slide up to the A-flat; attack it dead center:

A-cer - ba vo-lut-tà, dol - ce tor - tu - ra,

"In 'lentissima / agonia' make certain we hear those two a's that come together. Think of the phrase being notated like this:

len - tis - si - ma a - go - ni - a,

"There are many low-lying passages in this aria, and they must be forward and not woolly in sound or they will be lost. You can't sing each one in chest, however; I would save full chest for the end of the opening section—the word 'l'attesa':

ad a - mo - ro - so sen__ tor - na l'at - te - sa!

"When the Principessa comes in after the orchestra's largo, it should be at the first tempo. Watch the two *o*'s of 'eco, ogni'; let's hear both:

O - gni e - co o - gni om - bra

This entire section should drive in a headlong way; don't hold back, especially at the end before the orchestral interlude. If you do, the aria begins to fall apart when it should rage:

"The next section—con moto—is like recitative. Move through it quickly and rhythmically, then pause and breathe well before beginning the lyrical section, 'O vagabonda stella.' This rich section should be as legato and even as possible, but keep the pulse of passion underneath:

"When you come to the high A, go straight up to it; don't drag. At the very end, give yourself enough breath and room to build as big a crescendo as possible so that the aria will finish with the maximum of effect. Save enough for a final surge at the end, but do not end with the *r* sound of 'amor.' End instead with the power of your diaphragm. The secret is to always save a little breath in reserve for that last push:

EPILOGUE

"I am not good with words, but there is one thing I would ask of you: that our efforts not be wasted, that you do not forget what little I have given you. Take it and apply it to other scores, so that your phrasing, your diction, your knowledge, and your courage will be stronger—especially your courage. Do not think singing is an easy career. It is a lifetime's work; it does not stop here. As future colleagues, you must carry on. Fight bad tradition; remember, we are servants to those better than us—the composers. They believed; we must believe.

"Of course, by helping the composer we help ourselves. But this takes courage—the courage to say no to easy applause, to fireworks for their own sake. You must know what you want to do in life, you must decide, for we cannot do everything. Everyone seems in a hurry today—too much so, I think. Conductors frequently do not have the time to know what these scores are about. You must show them in a nice way what is necessary for the composer and why. This is what I have always tried to do, and what I have wanted to instill in you who will follow.

"Whether I continue singing or not doesn't matter. What matters is that you use whatever you have learned wisely. Think of the expression of the words, of good diction, and of your own deep feelings. The only thanks I ask is that you sing properly and honestly. If you do this, I will feel repaid."

March 16, 1972

GLOSSARY

A piacere	At pleasure; a variance from strict tempo or rhythm	Assai	Enough
A piena voce	In full voice	Bel canto	"Beautiful singing"; a lyrical, fluid vocal style of the mid-seventeenth to mid-nineteenth centuries
A tempo	In tempo		
Abellimento(-i)	Embellishment(s)		
Accelerando	Getting faster		
Accento(-i)	Accent(s)		
Acciaccatura(-e)	Ornamental, nonharmonic note(s); unmeasured note (a grace note)	Brillante	Brilliantly
		Brio	Spirit, liveliness
		Cabaletta	A second aria which usually follows a cavatina and is most often brilliant and in a fast tempo
Adagio	Smoothly; a slow tempo		
Affettuoso(-a)	Affectionate, loving		
Affrettare	To hurry	Cadenza	An ornamental passage at a cadence, usually without accompaniment
Agitato; agitatissimo	Agitated; very agitated		
Allargando	Broadening		
Allegretto	A moderate tempo	Calmo(-a)	Calm
Allegro	Cheerful; a quick tempo	Cantabile	Singing (adj.); a singing, lyrical passage
Andante; andantino	A relaxed, walking tempo	Cavatina	A type of aria, usually reflective, lyrical, and in a slow tempo
Angoscia	Anguish		
Anima	Soul	Con	With
Animato; animando	Animated; animating	Crescendo(-i); crescendissimo	Growing louder; growing as loud as possible
Appena	Slightly		
Appoggiato(-a)	Leaned upon		
Appoggiatura(-e)	Ornamental, nonharmonic note(s) with a measured value, as opposed to the unmeasured acciaccatura	Declamando	Declaring
		Decrescendo	Growing softer
		Diminuendo(-i)	Diminishing
		Dolce; dolcissimo	Sweet; sweetest
		Dolore	Sadness
Arpeggio	A spread or broken chord in which the notes are sounded separately	Espansione	Expansion
		Espansivo	Expansive
		Espressivo	Expressive

Fermata(-e)	Stop(s) or hold(s)	Piano; pianissimo	Soft; softest
Fil di voce	A thread of voice	Più	More
Fioritura(-e)	Flowerlike; ornamental passage(s)	Poco (poco a poco)	Little (little by little)
Forte; fortissimo	Loud; loudest	Portamento(-i)	Carried; slur(s) between two notes
Forza	Force	Portando	Carrying, slurring
Giusto	Exact	Presto; prestissimo	A very quick tempo; the very quickest tempo
Glissando(-i); glissato	Sliding; slid		
Grande; grandioso	Grand or large; full of grandeur	Quasi	Somewhat
		Rallentando	Slowing down
Grazia	Grace	Recitativo(-i)	Recitation(s); speechlike passage(s), usually preceding an aria
Gruppettino(-i)	Small group(s) of ornamental notes; a turn		
		Rinforzando	Reinforcing
Gruppetto(-i)	Group(s) of ornamental notes, usually extended	Ritardando	Holding back
		Rubato(-i)	Robbed; give(s) and take(s) in the rhythmic pulse of an aria
Incalzando	Hastening, pressing		
Lacerante	Rending		
Lamento	Lament	Secco	Dry
Languore	Languor	Semplicità; semplicemente	Simplicity; simply
Larga la frase	Broaden the phrase		
Largo; larghetto	A broad tempo; broadly	Sempre	Always, ever
		Silenzio	Silence
Legato	Bound smoothly, without a break	Sostenuto	Sustained
		Sotto voce	Under the voice; a vocal aside
Legg(i)ero	Light		
Lento; lentamente	A slow tempo; slowly	Spinto	Pushed; a lyrical sound put to dramatic use
Lirico	Lyrical		
Lunga	Long	Staccato(-i)	Detached; lightly touched note(s)
Maestoso	Stately		
Marcato(-e)	Marked; accent(s)	Stato d'anima	State of soul or being
Massimo(-a)	Maximum	Stentare	To strive; to perform in a labored way
Meno	Less		
Messa di voce	Placing of the voice; a held note that is swelled and then diminished	Stesso	Same
		Stringendo	Squeezing; a gradual quickening of a tempo
		Tempo primo	The original speed; comes after new tempo indications have been introduced
Mezzo	Half		
Moderato	Moderate		
Modo	Manner, mode		
Molto	Very	Tenuto	Held
Morendo	Dying away	Triste	Sad
Mosso	Moved; quicker	Tutto	All
Moto	Motion	Valzer	Waltz
Movimento	Movement	Verismo	A realistic, true-to-life operatic style of the late nineteenth and early twentieth centuries
Parlato	Spoken		
Passaggio	Passage; a place where the voice makes a transition from one register to another		
		Vivace	Vivacious
		Vivo	Lively